Management Practices
for the
Health Professional

Third Edition

Beaufort B. Longest, Jr.
Graduate School of Public Health
University of Pittsburgh

RESTON PUBLISHING COMPANY, INC.
A Prentice-Hall Company
Reston, Virginia

Library of Congress Cataloging in Publication Data

Longest, Beaufort B.
    Management practices for the health professional.

    Includes bibliogaphical references and index.
    1. Health services administration.   2. Management.
I. Title.
RA393.L66 1984   362.1'068   83-17826
ISBN 0-8359-4191-4

Editorial/production supervision and
interior design by Camelia Townsend

10   9   8   7   6   5   4   3   2   1

PRINTED IN THE UNITED STATES OF AMERICA

For Carolyn,

*Whose presence in my life has
made many things possible—
and doing them seem worthwhile.*

Contents

Preface

The publication of a new edition of a book suggests two things: something about earlier editions stimulated enough interest to make the book at least a commercial success and the subject matter of the book must have changed enough to warrant the revision and updating necessary for a new edition. Both of these conditions apply to this book.

The first edition (1976) was written for a particular group of people—health professionals who find themselves in positions of managerial responsibility. They are at the epicenter of many problems the health care system faces. They continued to be the intended audience for the second edition in 1980; now, more than ever, they are the audience for this new edition. These men and women, collectively, guide a vital and very expensive industry. An understanding of their roles as managers and of the organizations in which they play their roles is crucial to their effective performance. This book will provide information and insights that will enhance the skills of practicing managers and lay a foundation for students who will someday assume managerial roles. We do not purport to give the reader all that he or she needs to know about management, but to provide a foundation of understanding upon which to build as the health professional learns to practice his or her profession in relation to, and (more and more) dependent on, other people in an organizational context.

Today's health services are increasingly being delivered in an organizational setting. The complexity of modern health service delivery requires, to a greater extent than ever, an organizational setting. Much health service delivery must be supported by the skills, technology, and physical facilities that only an organizational setting can provide. This is not a new trend, but it has been gaining considerable momentum in recent years. The number of specialties with highly developed training has increased, as have the physical aspects of technology, facilities, and equipment. Thus, it is critically important for those who deliver or help to deliver health services (the health professionals) to understand not only their professional areas of expertise but the complexities of organization theory and management as they relate to the *organized* delivery of health services.

The format of this edition has remained unchanged. However, many chapters have been substantially rewritten to reflect the changes that have occurred in the health care field and in the knowledge base upon which the management process is built. The vignette that opens each chapter is intended to illustrate the nature of management problems toward which the information in each chapter is directed. The vignettes all pertain to the untimely death of a fictitious patient in a hypothetical hospital. Even so, the problems contained in the vignettes are common to a great many health services organizations.

A special note of appreciation is due Ms. Donna J. Lee, my administrative assistant, for her tireless efforts in getting the revised manuscript in suitable form and for holding me to the necessary schedule in the writing task. The efforts of Ms. Camelia Townsend in managing the editing and production of this revision are greatly appreciated.

I would also like to thank my sons, Brant and Courtland, who many times during the preparation of this manuscript went outside with me to play, thus refreshing my mind for the challenge of this revision. I want them to know that our time together never interferes with my work—although sometimes my work interferes with our time together.

Beaufort B. Longest, Jr.

Modern Health Services
in an
Organized Setting

ONE

The brightly lit cafeteria, filled with the smell of fresh coffee, was like a little island to the day shift employees of Memorial Hospital as they shook off the chill of a March wind and drank their first cup of coffee before the work day began.

At one table, several people were talking about the circumstances surrounding the death of Mr. Luther J. Fillerey.

"It's a mystery to me," the Chief Resident (who had led the resuscitation team) said between gulps of coffee. "I was called around 2:00 a.m. and told that he was going sour. His fever spiked to 104° and his breathing was very labored."

"What time did he arrest?" asked the Head Nurse for the day shift on the unit where Mr. Fillerey had been a patient.

"A little after three o'clock. I'm not sure exactly, but we declared him dead at 3:54 this morning. We worked on him for almost an hour. For a while there it looked like he might make it—but in the end we couldn't bring him around," the Chief Resident replied, his eyes never leaving his coffee.

"It's a shame," murmured one of the Student Nurses who had been assigned to Mr. Fillerey's floor.

"Sure it's a shame," the Head Nurse shot back, "but people die in hospitals!"

The Student Nurse glanced toward the Head Nurse and said, "But he was a young man, early thirties maybe, and quite pleasant to be around—at least up until the last few days—it seems so senseless. We have all this technology and all these people here, and still people die."

One of the Medical Technologists who had been sitting at the table stood up quickly saying, "Look at the time—we'd better get down to the lab and pick up our requisitions and get some blood drawn!" She and another Technologist left together.

The Head Nurse touched the Student's hand and said, "We'd better go, too." They left the Chief Resident still staring into his coffee. It was 7:25 a.m.

INTRODUCTION

The last half century of unparalleled progress in the scientific and technological base of medicine has brought a fundamental change in the way health services are delivered. This change, which affects every health professional in every developed country on earth, is that so much of the delivery of health services must now occur within the context of an organization. These organizations serve to bring together the human, technological, and physical resources that make the practice of modern medicine possible. Thus, it is critically important that those who are, or plan to be, health professionals understand not only their professional area of expertise but also the nature of the organizations in which they will practice their professions.

Further, since many health professionals are, or will be, managers in these organizations, it is necessary for them to understand the practice of management. The purpose of this chapter is to describe the organizational context of health services. Then we can turn our attention, in the remaining chapters, to the practice of management within these organizations.

The description of the organizational context of modern medicine is a complex task. The scope of the subject is broad and dynamic; in essence, we must describe the U.S. health care system. Before we do, three definitions are needed. First, *health* has been defined by the World Health Organization as a state of "complete physical, mental, and social well-being and not merely the absence of disease." From this lofty ideal, the World Health Organization has tried to give meaning to the term *health* by setting as a goal "the attainment by all citizens of the world by the year 2000 of a level of health that will permit them to lead a socially and economically productive life." Health or health status in a human being is a function of many factors including the basic biological characteristics and processes that comprise human biology (some diseases are inherited); the conditions external to the body (some diseases are caused by or exacerbated by environmental conditions); and the behavior patterns that constitute lifestyle (some diseases result from the pattern or style of life). The World Health Organization's definition of health describes an ideal state—one that is impossible to measure; yet it represents a target that permits a definition of a second important term.

Dictionaries generally define service as "an act of helpful activity." Thus *health services*, in their simplest terms, are acts of helpful activity specifically intended to maintain or improve health. Health services can be divided into three basic types: public health services, which are activities that must be conducted on a community basis such as communicable disease control and the collection and analysis of health statistics; environmental health services, which often overlap with public health services and include such activities as insect and rodent control and air pollution control; and personal health services, which are activities directed at individuals and include promotion of health, prevention of illness, diagnosis, treatment (sometimes leading to a cure), and rehabilitation. Helpful activities as diverse as the delicate corneal transplant performed on a sixty-year-old woman, the drainage of a swamp in Louisiana during mosquito season, the counseling of an obese member of an HMO, and the separation of smokers and nonsmokers on a commercial airliner are all health services.

Building on these definitions, it is possible to define the *health care system* as the resources (money, people, physical plant, and technology) and the organizational configurations necessary to transform these resources into health services. It is the "acts of helpful activity specifically intended to maintain or improve health" that form the ultimate purpose of the health care system; the accessibility, quality, appropriateness, and efficiency of these health services should constitute the basis of fair and rational judgments about the health care system.

It is important to note that the health care system and the services it provides are only one of a set of factors that affect health status. Figure 1–1 represents, through the relative size of the arrows, assumptions about the relative importance of these determinants of health status. Thus, for example, when a man with a family history of (genetic tendency toward) cancer smokes heavily, lives in a polluted urban environment, sees a physician long after symptoms emerge, and subsequently dies of lung cancer, the death of this man is not a fair and rational basis upon which to judge the health care system inadequate. The death of an infant whose mother could not get good prenatal care (accessibility), the unnecessary surgery performed by a less than fully qualified surgeon (appropriateness and quality), and the patient who pays a grossly inflated price for a diagnostic procedure because the

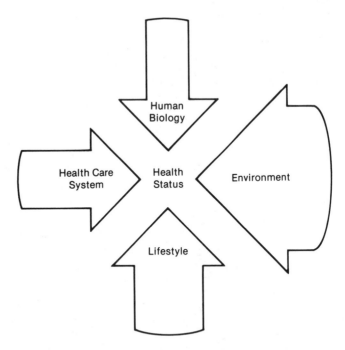

Figure 1–1. Determinants of health status.

SOURCE: This figure is similar to one developed by Henrik L. Blum, *Planning for Health; Development and Application of Social Change Theory* (New York: Human Sciences Press, 1973), p. 3. Reprinted with permission.

machine necessary to conduct the procedure is owned by a hospital in a town where too many such machines exist (efficiency) are fairer and more rational bases upon which to judge that the health care system is inadequate.

Ironically, expenditures on health services, especially at the federal level, are not at all consistent with the view of the determinants of health status represented in Figure 1–1. Figure 1–2 depicts a rough estimate of the distribution of federal health expenditures by these determinants. This paradox between determinants of health and expenditures for health is not likely to change dramatically in the years immediately ahead. The historical causes of the paradox are far too complex to explore in detail here. Yet, it serves to put the discussion of the health care system in the United States in proper perspective: the health care system absorbs the vast majority of dollars spent to affect health status, but it is increasingly seen to be very limited in terms of future positive impact on the status of health of the U.S. population.

This is not to say that the health care system is not important to health status. It is after all the source of intervention when illness

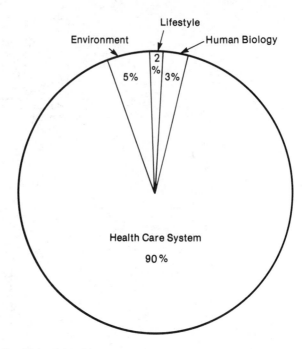

Figure 1–2. Federal health expenditures by health determinant (estimated).

or disease occurs even though their roots may lie in environmental, biological, or behavioral determinants. In this sense, the health care system can be viewed as a line of defense against the awful toll of untreated environmentally, biologically, and/or behaviorally caused illness and disease. It is largely because preventive measures in the areas of environmental, biological, and behavioral determinants have been neither sufficient nor effective that the health care system is so vital to maintaining, to say nothing of improving, the health status of the U.S. population. With this perspective as background, we can turn to a description of the health care system.

THE DYNAMICS OF THE HEALTH CARE SYSTEM

The resources—money, people, physical plant, and technology—and the organizational configurations necessary to transform them into health services are described in the sections that follow. Also, consideration will be given to the problems confronting the system as it attempts to provide services that are simultaneously of high quality, appropriate, efficiently produced, and accessible to all who need them. First of all, however, it is important to recognize the dynamic nature of the U.S. health care system. The dynamics are nowhere more explicit than in numbers of dollars spent. In 1984, total health expenditures are climbing past the $400 billion level. They are expected to reach more than $750 billion and be about 11.5% of GNP by 1990. This is up from $245 billion in 1980 and only $75 billion in 1970. These dramatic increases reflect several things—not only inflation and increased utilization but also growth and change in the system.

The changes in the health care system reflect social change, different priorities, new technology, more regulation of the system, changes in disease trends, new delivery methods, and new approaches to paying for health care. All of these factors contribute to the dynamic state of the U.S. health care system. For example, there have been significant increases in drug addiction (particularly alcoholism) and venereal disease in recent years. Increasingly, these problems are viewed as health problems rather than social or criminal problems and thus bring concomitant increased expectation that the health care system should provide solutions. The president of one of the nation's leading health care organizations has summarized the impact of new technology by pointing out that "one of the significant results of advances in medical technology has been greater specialization of facilities, equipment, and personnel. This specialization has led to a decline in the number of general or primary care practitioners, has increased fragmentation of the delivery of care, and has produced a greater need for coordination of the various components of the delivery process."[1]

When the effects of similar factors are considered, the dynamic nature of the health care system begins to come into focus.

RESOURCES IN THE HEALTH CARE SYSTEM

The U.S. health care system, ultimately devoted to the provision of health services, requires an enormous quantity and variety of resources. Resources are defined here simply as the basic building blocks of the system: money, people, physical plant, and technology.

---

[1]James A. Campbell and Richard G. DuFour, "Organization of Hospital Resources," in *Hospitals in the 1980's* (Chicago: American Hospital Association, 1977), p. 9.

Money

As already noted, the health care system requires a total expenditure of about $400 billion dollars annually and consumes about 10 percent of the nation's gross national product (GNP). Figure 1–3 illustrates the trend of this growth in total expenditures and Figure 1–4 illustrates the trend in share of GNP. As Figures 1–5 and 1–6 illustrate, a substantial part of the nation's health expenditures are for hospital care and physicians' services. These and other forms of personal health services are paid for in one of four basic ways:

1. Direct, or "out-of-pocket," payment in which an individual pays for his care directly from his own funds.
2. Private insurance in which an individual or someone on his behalf, such as an employer, enters into a contractual arrangement with an insurer who agrees to pay for a specified

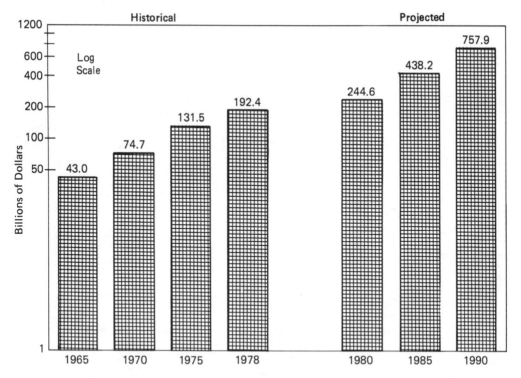

Figure 1–3. Total national health expenditures, selected years 1965 to 1990.

SOURCE: Office of Research, Demonstrations, and Statistics. Health Care Financing Administration

Reported in Mark Freeland, et al., "Projections of National Health Expenditures, 1980, 1985, 1990," *Health Care Financing Review* Vol. 1, No. 3 (Winter 1980).

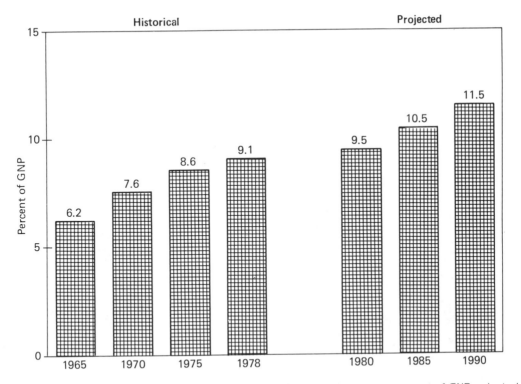

Figure 1–4. Total national health expenditures as a percent of GNP, selected years 1965 to 1990.

SOURCE: Office of Research, Demonstrations, and Statistics. Health Care Financing Administration

Reported in Mark Freeland, et al., "Projections of National Health Expenditures, 1980, 1985, 1990," *Health Care Financing Review* Vol. 1, No. 3 (Winter 1980).

set of services under specified conditions in return for premium payments; or a prepayment is made to a provider such as a health maintenance organization or an organization such as Blue Cross who then contracts with providers to provide services to subscribers.

3. Government programs, principally Medicare, in which the federal government pays for health care services provided to social security recipients over age 65, and Medicaid, in which federal funds are combined with state funds to pay for health care services received by welfare recipients and other people, defined by state law, to be medically indigent. Payments under both Medicare and Medicaid are made to providers of service on behalf of program beneficiaries.

4. Although the relative amount is decreasing, some care is paid for through charitable contributions, endowment funds, or

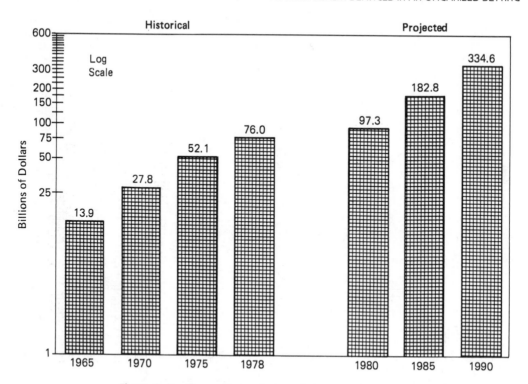

Figure 1–5. Expenditures for hospital care, selected years 1965 to 1990.

SOURCE: Office of Research, Demonstrations, and Statistics. Health Care Financing Administration

Reported in Mark Freeland, et al., "Projections of National Health Expenditures, 1980, 1985, 1990," *Health Care Financing Review* Vol. 1, No. 3 (Winter 1980).

revenue generated by providers from other sources of income such as hospital parking lots. All but the first of these mechanisms of payment are termed "third-party payments" because the providers of health care services receive payment from a source other than directly from the individual who received the care. Direct, out-of-pocket payment now accounts for only about one-third of total expenditures for personal health care services. The complex flow of funds for the payment for health care services in the United States is shown in Figure 1–7.

People

Another basic building block of the health care system is manpower. The Department of Labor lists more than 225 categories of workers who are employed primarily in the health care system.

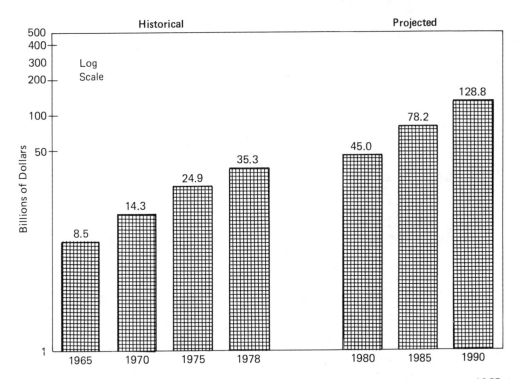

Figure 1–6. Expenditures for physicians' services, selected years 1965 to 1990.

SOURCE: Office of Research, Demonstrations, and Statistics. Health Care Financing Administration

Reported in Mark Freeland, et al., "Projections of National Health Expenditures, 1980, 1985, 1990," *Health Care Financing Review* Vol. 1, No. 3 (Winter 1980).

(Rounded numbers are used throughout this section.) About 5 million people work in the health care system. There are now about 431,000 active physicians, 1,225,000 registered nurses and 380,000 practical nurses, 131,000 dentists, 135,000 pharmacists and 534,000 technologists and technicians at work in the U.S. health care system.

The training of health manpower occurs in a wide variety of educational settings. There is an extensive program of certification and licensure designed to ensure the competence of health manpower. Certification is granted by a variety of organizations and/or the states to people who meet certain requirements established for many health care occupations. Certification does not exclude others from working in that occupation. Licensure is a good deal stronger in that it is a recognition of competence granted by the states. Without a license, pharmacists, physicians, professional nurses, dentists, and optometrists, among other health profes-

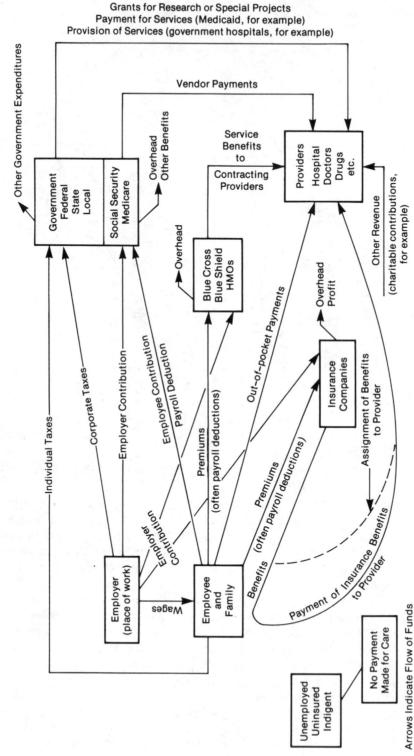

Figure 1–7. Flow of funds for payment of health care services in the U.S.

Arrows Indicate Flow of Funds

SOURCE: Florence A. Wilson and Duncan Neuhauser, *Health Services in the United States* (Cambridge, MA: Ballinger Publishing Co., 1974). p. 91. Reprinted with permission from *Health Services in the United States*, Copyright 1974, Ballinger Publishing Company.

sionals, cannot practice their profession. Licensure and certification represent attempts to ensure the availability of health manpower resources with acceptable levels of preparation. In addition, these programs tend to restrict the supply of health manpower and thus drive up the cost of this critical resource of the health care system.

Physical Plant

Another building block of the health care system is the nation's investment in the "bricks and mortar" of physical facilities required to meet health care needs. (Rounded numbers are used throughout this section.)

There are almost 7,000 hospitals in the U.S. health care system, with more than 1.3 million beds. On any given day, about 1.1 million people are patients in the nation's hospitals, and more than 270 million outpatient visits occur annually.[2] Table 1–1 shows trends in hospitals, beds, and admissions for selected years. It is

TABLE 1–1 *Total United States Hospitals, Beds, Admissions.*

	1950	1960	1970	1980	1981	1982
Hospitals	6,788	6,876	7,123	6,965	6,933	6,915
Beds (in thousands)	1,456	1,658	1,616	1,365	1,362	1,360
Admissions (in thousands)	18,483	25,027	31,759	38,892	39,169	39,095

Note: Total hospitals include the following: federal, non-federal psychiatric, non-federal tuberculosis and other respiratory diseases, non-federal long-term general and other special, and non-federal short-term general and other special.

SOURCE: *Hospital Statistics,* 1983 edition, Chicago: American Hospital Association.

important to recognize that there is substantial variation in U.S. hospitals in terms of size, scope of service, ownership, and other characteristics. The American Hospital Association's Annual Publication, *Hospital Statistics,* provides a wealth of statistical information on U.S. hospitals.

There are now about 20,000 nursing homes with 4 million beds in the United States. The federal government recognizes three categories of nursing homes based on the type of service they provide: skilled nursing facilities (SNF), which provide continuous nursing service on a 24-hour basis; intermediate care facilities

---

[2]American Hospital Association, *Hospital Statistics* (Chicago: American Hospital Association, 1982), p. 7.

(ICF); and residential facilities, called rest homes. About 8.4% of the national health expenditures are for nursing home care.

Another major category of physical plant resources in the health care system is represented by the facilities necessary for the office practices of the nation's physicians. A great deal of personal medical care is rendered in physicians' offices. About 80% of physicians are engaged in the direct care of patients as their primary activity. Of these, approximately 70% are engaged in office-based practice and 30% are in hospital-based practice. While the majority of office-based physicians are in solo practice, i.e., independent practice by a physician usually with his own facilities and equipment, many physicians are in group practices (three or more physicians formally organized to provide medical care, consultation, diagnosis, and/or treatment through the joint use of equipment and personnel and with income from medical practice distributed in accordance with methods previously determined by members of the group). These groups may be organized as general practice, single specialty, or multi-specialty groups. The physical facilities necessary to support physicians in office practices represent a substantial investment in physical plant.

While all of the physical plant resources of the health care system are too numerous to even mention here, some of its other components include about 13,000 ambulance services and 2,800 medical laboratories independent of those in physician's offices and hospitals. In addition there are about 9,000 commercial dental laboratories, and about 90% of the nation's active dentists are in private office practices.

Technology

The technological base of modern medicine is truly remarkable and must be viewed as one of the building blocks of the health care system. It has made organ transplants and microscopic surgery possible; many diseases have been eradicated and treatment for others has been greatly improved; and early diagnosis for many diseases has been possible. These advances have had a marked impact on the health care system: diseases are treated that once were not even diagnosed, societal expectations of the health care system have risen (often unrealistically) as technology has advanced, and the costs of health care have risen dramatically as expensive new technology has been adopted.

The paradox of technological advance is that as people benefit from it (live longer) they are then in a position to need and utilize other health services; the net effect is to drive up total health care expenditures. This phenomenon becomes important, even critical, when it occurs in a context of limited dollars for health care expenditures. The result is complex and frustrating. As one authority has said, "If someone told me ten years ago that now that we have a way to arrest death from kidney disease that ... we'd be fighting over how to pay for it, I wouldn't have believed it."[3] Yet, this is precisely the problem that technology presents the health care system today. It is likely now that as new technology is developed its adoption will be carefully weighed in terms of its relative cost against projected benefits—a new *modus operandi* for the health care system.

It is clear that the health care system is structured from building blocks that include vast sums of money, many different kinds of people with specialized training, an impressive investment in physical plant, and a growing technology. In the next section, we turn our attention to some of the organizations that these resources have been used to build and maintain and that, in turn, convert these resources into health services.

ORGANIZATIONS IN THE HEALTH CARE SYSTEM

The organizations within it are the most visible part of the health care system. There are thousands of organizations, and they give form and substance to the system. The variety of these organizations defies easy categorization. Figure 1–8, however, can serve as a starting point for their description. The shortcomings of such a

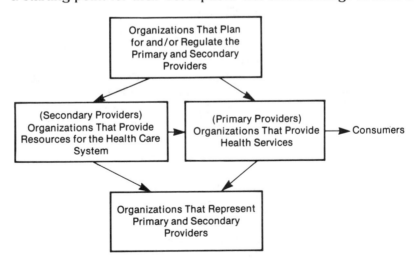

Figure 1–8. Organizations in the health care system.

[3]Belding Scribner, Personal Interview described in R. Fox and J. P. Swazey, *The Courage to Fail* (Chicago: University of Chicago Press, 1974), p. 329.

categorization become apparent quickly when one considers, for example, that Blue Cross plans, which are primarily providers of a basic resource (payment for services rendered to its subscribers), sometimes *require* hospitals that receive payment from them to prove the need for expansion of services, and Blue Cross plans typically have representatives on areawide planning boards. These activities could qualify them as a planning and regulating organization. Or consider the case of a hospital, whose primary purpose is the provision of health care services, but which also operates a school of nursing; or the medical school that operates a hospital. It is not always easy to categorize organizations in the health care system.

Organizations That Provide Health Services

This category of primary providers includes the following kinds of organizations: hospitals, nursing homes, physician's offices, health maintenance organizations, home care programs, clinics, and local health departments, among others. Their distinguishing characteristic is that they provide the physical plant where the delivery of health care services is made directly to consumers whether the purpose of those services is curative, preventive, or rehabilatative. Three of these primary provider organizations are described in some detail below.

Hospitals

Hospitals are perhaps the most complex organizations in the health care system. They come in many types and sizes but by definition a hospital is "a health care institution with an organized medical and professional staff, and with permanent facilities that include inpatient beds, that provides medical, nursing, and other health related services to patients."[4] A general hospital will usually be organized along the lines shown in Figure 1–9, although the reader should be cautioned that hospitals will almost invariably differ in details of their organization. The functions of the general hospital have been described as follows:

> First, there are diagnostic and treatment services to inpatients. Within this broad function are many subdivisions of medical, surgical, obstetrical, pediatric, and other special forms of care. Psychiatric service and rehabilitation may be included. Involved in all of these inpatient services are various modalities, including nursing, dietetics, pharmaceutical skills, laboratory and X-ray services, and varying refinements of diagnosis and therapy. Second, there are services to

---

[4]American Hospital Association, *Hospital Administration Terminology* (Chicago: American Hospital Association, 1982), p. 17.

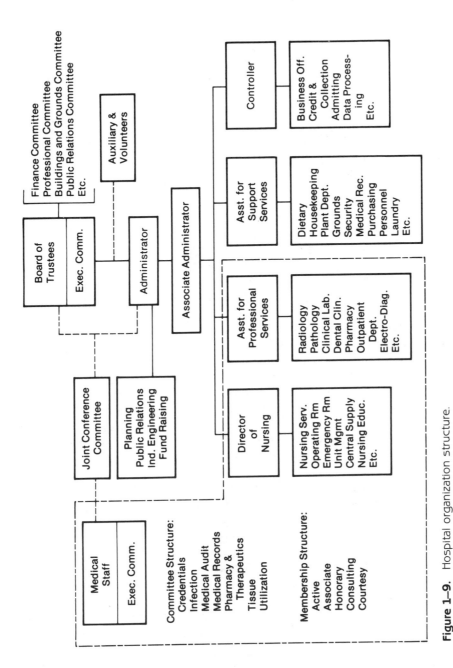

Figure 1–9. Hospital organization structure.

SOURCE: *A Primer for Hospital Trustees* (Washington: Chamber of Commerce of the United States, 1974), p. 31.

outpatients, with an equally wide range of specialties and technical modalities. A third hospital function concerns professional and technical education, for many classes of health personnel must work in hospitals and thereby receive training. A fourth function is medical research, since the accumulation of patients in hospitals provides the basis for scientific investigation into the causes, diagnosis, and treatment of diseases. A fifth function concerns prevention of diseases or health promotion in the surrounding population; there are many ways that hospitals, as centers for technical skill, can offer services to people before they are sick or can protect patients from the hazards of disease beyond that for which they have come to the hospital.[5]

The emphasis given to these various functions will vary from hospital to hospital, depending largely upon the basic objectives and goals of the particular hospital. For example, the large medical center may emphasize education and research to a much greater extent than the small general hospital.

The hospital is a very complex social system with substantial conflicts among the participants—patients, physicians, trustees, administrative staff, and other personnel. The diversity of the organization creates major problems. The governing board has the legal authority over, and responsibility for, the organization. The medical staff possesses the technical knowledge to make decisions regarding patient care and treatment. The administrative staff is responsible for day-to-day functioning of the hospital. These three elements, sometimes referred to as the organizational triad, share the same basic objectives. However, each element of the triad must interpret the means for meeting these objectives in terms of its own values and personalities, which are not identical. This makes the hospital one of the most complex institutions in modern society.

Nursing Homes   Since the enactment of the Social Security Act of 1935, which made public assistance funds available for the needy aged, the nursing home industry has flourished in the United States. Several other factors have exacerbated the need for institutional care for the aged. Among them, and perhaps most important, are the increased percentage of older people (65+) in the population and changes in the family structure. The nursing home is defined as an "institution with an organized professional staff and permanent facilities, including inpatient beds, that provides continuous nursing and other health-related, psychological, and personal services to patients who are not in an acute phase of illness but who primarily require continued care on an inpatient basis."[6]

---

[5]Milton I. Roemer and J. W. Friedman, *Doctors in Hospitals* (Baltimore: The Johns Hopkins Press, 1971), pp. 1-2.

[6]American Hospital Association, *Hospital Administration Terminology*, p. 27.

The nursing home serves several basic health care functions. Among them are the following:

1. To provide continuing care for those recovering from surgical or medical disorders.
2. To assist patients in reaching optimal physical and emotional health.
3. To provide for the total needs of patients—physical, emotional, and spiritual.
4. To assist the aging toward an active participation in life.
5. To provide for rehabilitative services when the need exists.
6. To work cooperatively with other community and social agencies.[7]

The typical organization pattern of the nursing home is very similar to that given for the hospital, the main difference being that the nursing home offers a much narrower range of services. A second major difference is a less complex medical staff organization in the nursing home where medical staff are not as involved in day-to-day patient care. A typical nursing home organization is shown in Figure 1–10. The reader is cautioned that, as with hospitals, there are many alternative patterns of organization.

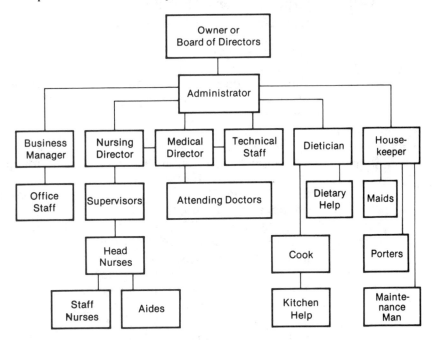

Figure 1–10. Nursing home organization structure.

[7]Florence L. McQuillan, *Fundamentals of Nursing Home Administration*, 2nd ed. (Philadelphia: W. B. Saunders Company, 1974), p. 3.

**Health
Maintenance
Organiza-
tions—
HMOs**

While the hospital and the nursing home represent two of the most important traditional health service provider organizations, there are new types of organizations that fit this category. Few subjects have aroused more interest or generated more discussion in the health care community during the past few years than the concept of health maintenance organizations—or, as they are more commonly called, "HMOs."

> There are five essential features of an HMO. Each single component or feature does not make the HMO special but, taken together, the five components make the HMO a unique form of health care delivery. An HMO is an *organized system* providing a comprehensive range of health care services to a *voluntarily enrolled* consumer population. In return for a *prepaid, fixed fee,* the enrollee is guaranteed a defined set of *benefits*. This fixed fee is usually the same for all members (enrollees) of the HMO regardless of the extent of services utilized. The prospective enrollee usually has a dual choice of joining either an HMO delivery system or another form of health insurance (e.g. Blue Cross/Blue Shield or commercial insurance policy). Enrollees join the HMO primarily on a year-to-year (contractual) basis and have the option of changing their choice once a year."[8]

Organizations That Provide Resources for the Health Care System

This category of secondary providers includes educational institutions, financing mechanisms, and drug and equipment suppliers, among others. Their distinguishing characteristic is that they provide resources needed for the direct provision of health services.

**Educational
Institutions**

Space does not permit a description of the tremendous variety of educational organizations that supply health manpower. The medical schools and the nursing schools are perhaps the dominant examples, but all of the educational organizations make an impact on the health care system.

Physicians, still the key manpower in the health care system, are trained in the nation's 125 medical schools, or they are trained in foreign medical schools. Foreign medical graduates (FMGs) now represent about 20% of the total active physicians in this country. While there is considerable variation among U.S. medical schools in terms of curriculum, they generally provide four years of post-baccalaureate training consisting of two years of preclinical, or basic sciences work, and two years of clinical and practical experience.

---

[8]U.S. Department of Health and Human Services, *A Student's Guide to Health Maintenance Organizations* (Washington: U.S. Department of HHS, 1978), p. 5.

The present mold for medical education was largely cast in the 1910 document written by Abraham Flexner, *Medical Education in the United States and Canada, A Report to the Carnegie Foundation for the Advancement of Teaching*, which criticized (well deserved) extant medical schools and led to major improvements. Following medical school, physicians enter a period of graduate medical education called residency. This education lasts two to seven years depending upon the specialty chosen.

The physician who wishes, after specialty training, can apply to be certified in that specialty by a specialty board. After meeting the requirements (which generally include completion of an approved residency, written and oral examination, and varying years of experience), the physician becomes a board certified specialist. This certification is in addition to licensure, which is granted by each state and which requires graduating from an approved medical school and passing an examination as set forth in each state's Medical Practice Act. Many states have reciprocity agreements with other states through which a physician may move his license from one state to another. The arduous path through a medical education serves not only to impart necessary knowledge but also to instill a distinctive group identity and, for many physicians, a rather homogenous set of values.

Professionally licensed nurses, usually called registered nurses (RNs), are trained in three different types of organizational settings: baccalaureate programs, which are four- or five-year university-based programs leading to a bachelor of science degree; associate degree programs, which are two-year programs usually based in junior or community colleges; and diploma programs, which usually provide three years of training past high school and are based in hospital-operated schools of nursing. Following completion of one of these approved programs, the nurse can become a registered nurse by passing a state licensure examination. There are also master's degree programs that provide nurses with advanced training in education, administration, or such clinical nursing specialties as public health, medical-surgical nursing, mental health, maternal and child health, and cardiovascular nursing. Other specialty training includes nurse anesthetists, nurse midwives, and pediatric and family nurse practitioners. A pediatric nurse practitioner, for example, is a registered nurse who has received additional training permitting an expanded role in the care of children.

Organizations That Pay for Care

A second important category of organizations that provide resources for the health care system are those that pay for care. Except for "out-of-pocket" payments by individuals, health care in the United States is largely paid for through third parties. The current maze of third parties has been created fairly recently—since the Great Depression—and has grown largely in response to the rising cost of health care and the concurrent financial risk that individuals run if they make no provision through insurance or prepayment for protection against their potential health care costs. More than half the third party payments now come from two sources: Blue Cross Plans and the federal government (principally Medicare and Medicaid).

The Blue Cross organization began as a prepayment plan for hospital expenses for school teachers in Dallas, Texas, in 1929. The original plan provided 21 days of hospitalization for a prepayment of 50 cents a month. Today, there are about 70 Blue Cross organizations covering almost 84 million subscribers. Blue Shield organizations provide for prepayment of physician fees in a similar manner. There are now about 86 million people covered by 70 Blue Shield organizations (or "Plans" as they are typically called). The Blue Cross plans are linked together as members of the Blue Cross Association.[9]

One of the most important dates in history, in terms of understanding the U.S. health care system, is July 1, 1966. On that date the federal government initiated two programs that had their basis in the 1965 amendments to the Social Security Act. These amendments (Title XVIII—Health Insurance for the Aged and Title XIX—Grants to the States for Medical Assistance Programs), more commonly known as Medicare and Medicaid, were the culmination of many years of national debate. Although substantial changes have been made in the Medicare and Medicaid programs in the intervening years, they were at their inception and still are insurance mechanisms to help pay for the health care of the elderly and the poor. Together, these programs account for more than 30% of the revenues that flow into the nation's hospitals.

Medicare is made up of two parts: Part A, which is compulsory insurance for hospital care and related services for the U.S. population over age 65, and Part B, which is voluntary supplementary insurance to partially cover the costs of physician and surgeon fees, clinic visits, diagnostic and laboratory tests, and home health visits. Part A is financed through Social Security payroll taxes, and Part B is financed from premium payments by enrollees and matching general revenues.

Medicaid is a program through which the federal government provides a subsidy to the states, 50–85% of the total cost depending on per capita income in the state, to help participating states provide health insurance to their poor and near-poor population.

---

[9]Blue Cross Association, *Blue Cross Fact Book, 1977* (Chicago: Blue Cross Association, 1977), p. 2.

Each state administers its own Medicaid program under certain federal requirements. Certain basic services must be provided including: inpatient and outpatient hospital care, laboratory and X-ray services, skilled nursing services, home health care, physician services, and family planning services.

The private, or commercial as they are often called, insurance companies represent another component of the third party payors. There are several hundred private insurance companies in the U.S., including some major ones like Prudential, Equitable, Aetna, Metropolitan, and Connecticut General. These companies, through their policies, provide "protection by written contract against the hazards (in whole or in part) of the happenings of specified fortuitous events."[10] Although private insurance companies were initially reluctant to enter the health insurance market, the market created by the large industrial unions that grew up during World War II provided a sufficient stimulus for their entry and by carefully experience-rating the various groups they serve, they have been successful.

Pharmaceutical and Medical Supply Industries

A third category of resource-providing organizations to be described briefly here are those found in the pharmaceutical and medical supply industries. Currently, the national expenditures for drugs total more than $20 billion. This represents both prescription drugs (also called ethical drugs), which are sold by prescription written by a physician only, and non-prescription drugs (also called over-the-counter drugs), which are sold directly to the public and for which no prescription is necessary. The pharmaceutical manufacturers direct their advertising of prescription drugs to physicians and to a lesser extent to pharmacists, their advertising of non-prescription drugs to the general public. The organizations supplying prescription drugs spend a great deal of money advertising and promoting their products to physicians. Roughly, the amounts represent one out of four dollars made on the wholesale prices of their products and almost four times the amount they spend on research and development.[11] The research and development costs are themselves quite large due to the complexity of the search for new, effective drugs and the nature of the process of obtaining approval from the Food and Drug Administration before the new drug can be placed on the market. Even with high marketing and R & D costs, the pharmaceutical industry has consistently earned high profits. The pharmaceutical manufac-

---

[10]Health Insurance Institute, *Source Book of Health Insurance Data* (New York: Health Insurance Institute, yearly).

[11]J.L. Goddard, "The Medical Business," *The Scientific American*, September 1973, pp. 161-166.

turers who make and sell prescription drugs are represented by the Pharmaceutical Manufacturers Association. Some of the larger members include: Abbott, Baxter, Bristol Meyers, Johnson and Johnson, Eli Lilly, Miles Laboratories, Pfizer, Squibb, and Upjohn.

The organizations that manufacture and distribute medical supplies are as diverse as their products, which range from cottonballs to computerized axial tomography (CAT) scanners costing hundreds of thousands of dollars each and capable of producing remarkably informative "pictures" of the inside of the human body. There are more than 1,100 medical supply organizations in the United States ranging from very large firms such as American Hospital Supply Corporation to relatively small firms which specialize in a few products.

While space has not permitted a comprehensive view of all the organizations, the reader can see that a diverse and diffuse set of organizations provide the resources necessary to sustain the U.S. health care system.

Organizations That Plan for and/or Regulate the Primary and Secondary Providers

It is important to note that the title of this subsection does not include "the health care system." This choice of title was made to emphasize the point that no one, to date, plans for or regulates the health care system. Instead, planning and regulating occur for many components of the system, but not the system as a whole. This fact is, if nothing more, consistent with the pluralism that characterizes the system itself. While there is a good deal of internal self-regulation and self-planning in health care organizations—for example, hospitals can regulate their own performance through organizational policies and procedures—we shall look mainly at external regulation and planning; that is, those organizations that are separate from, but that regulate, the primary and secondary providers or plan for the provision of health services.

Voluntary Regulating Groups

Regulation of health care providers has historically been on a voluntary basis. The voluntary regulatory process does not carry the mandate of law. The best example of voluntary regulation, among many possible choices, is the Joint Commission on Accreditation of Hospitals (JCAH), which can trace its origin to a 1915 program of the American College of Surgeons and whose board now includes representation from the American Medical Association, American Hospital Association, American College of Surgeons, American College of Physicians, and, more recently, both the American Association of Homes for the Aging and the American Nursing Home Association. The JCAH, through established standards, accredits hospitals and nursing homes who voluntarily seek such accreditation and thus guides and directs (regulates) much of the operation of these providers.

The voluntary regulation of organizations that train health manpower is extensive. The following partial list of education programs and the agencies that accredit them, and thus regulate their activities to a large extent, illustrates this:

Educational Program	Accrediting Agency
Cytotechnology	Council on Medical Education of the American Medical Association (AMA) and the American Society of Clinical Pathologists
Dentistry	Commission on Accreditation of the American Dental Association
Dietetics	American Dietetic Association
Hospital Administration	Accrediting Commission on Education for Health Administration
Medical Records	Council on Medical Education of the AMA and the Committee on Education and Registration of the American Medical Record Association
Medical Technology	Council on Medical Education of the AMA and the American Society for Medical Technology
Medicine	Council on Medical Education of the AMA and the Association of American Medical Colleges
Professional Nursing	State government agencies and the National League for Nursing
Pharmacy	American Council on Pharmaceutical Education
Physical Therapy	Council on Medical Education of the AMA and the American Physical Therapy Association
Radiologic Technology	Council on Medical Education of the AMA, American College of Radiology, and the American Society of Radiologic Technologists

Federal Regulating Efforts

Although the level of voluntary regulation in the health care system has been and continues to be high, governmental involvement in planning for and regulating the quality, cost, availability, and delivery of health care services in the United States has increased dramatically in the past two decades, especially since the enactment of the Medicare and Medicaid programs in the mid-1960's.

With the enactment, in 1974, of the National Health Planning and Resources Development Act (PL 93-641) and its subsequent implementation, governmental efforts to regulate the health care system perhaps reached its zenith.

This legislation created Health Systems Agencies (HSAs), which are responsible for health planning at the local level. Their responsibilities include forecasting demand and developing areawide plans for services and facilities. In addition, PL 93-641 calls for the establishment of State Health Planning and Development Agencies (SHPDAs), which develop state health plans. The single strongest element in PL 93-641 is the requirement that all states enact certificate-of-need (CON) legislation that meets federal standards. This feature permits tighter control (regulation) of capital expenditures for many existing health care providers and restricts the addition of new capacity in places where it is not needed.

The long-term impact of PL 93-641 on the health care system may essentially be a subordination of the goals and plans of individual provider organizations to those of the larger health care system. Proposals by providers have to be based on more thorough needs analysis and cost justification. Planning by the individual provider organization must relate to the specific plans developed for its area by the local HSA.

The overall federal involvement in the health care system is largely centered in the massive (with a budget second only to the Department of Defense) Department of Health and Human Services (DHHS). Established in 1953, DHHS has undergone several major reorganizations. Figure 1–11 represents a highly abbreviated view of DHHS as it is currently structured.

State Regulating Aspects

State government (and those aspects delegated to counties, cities, and towns) involvement in the health care system is made through a very complex and ever changing variety of organizations and agencies that vary from one state to another. Some of this involvement is lodged in a department of public health but ranges from assurance of water quality to education of physicians in state supported medical schools. State governments are heavily involved in planning for and regulating the health care system. Their involvement in planning under PL 93-641, which mandates State Health Planning and Development Agencies, is extensive; states now have certificate-of-need legislation through which they control the investment in various components of the health care system. The regulatory involvement by the states includes licensing of many categories of health care workers and provider organizations

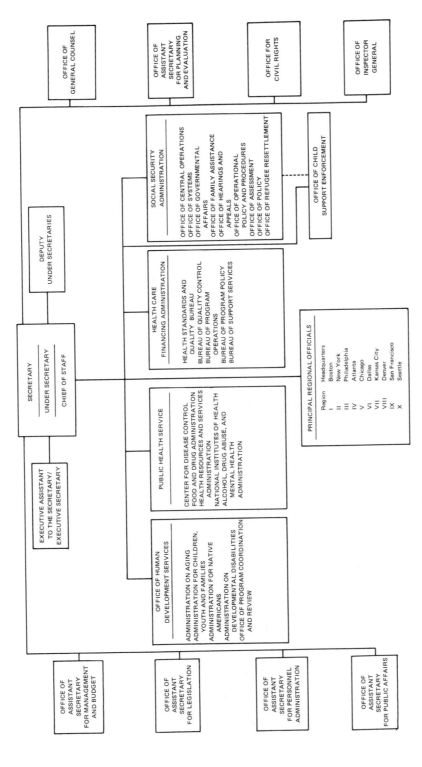

Figure 1-11. Summary of organization, Department of Health and Human Services.

SOURCE: U.S. Dept. HHS.

and the establishment and enforcement of insurance laws and health and safety codes. A final, and potentially very important, example of state regulatory involvement is rate review, already enacted in a number of states and being seriously considered in others. Under these programs the rates charged by providers for health services rendered are subject to review and approval by rate review agencies.

Two facts should be clear from this abbreviated description of organizations that regulate health care providers: (1) there is a tremendous amount of regulation of the system—it has been argued that the health care system is one of the most highly regulated components of the U.S. economy, and (2) there is a dramatic shift toward more governmental (especially federal) regulation of the health care system.

Organizations That Represent the Primary and Secondary Providers

The providers of health services, whether groups of individual professionals, such as physicians, dentists, nurses, and the many other categories of manpower, or the provider organizations, such as hospitals and nursing homes, are almost invariably represented by an association whose main purpose is to represent the interest of its constituency. In addition to national associations, such as the American Medical Association and the American Hospital Association, there are usually state associations, such as the Illinois Hospital Association and the Kentucky Medical Association, and frequently local organizations that represent the interests of members, such as the Prince George's County Medical Society and the Hospital Council of Western Pennsylvania.

As an example of one association, the American Dental Association can be described as "the national voluntary organization for the dental profession in the United States" with the formal objective "to encourage the improvement of the health of the public, to promote the art and science of dentistry and to represent the interests of the dental profession and the public which it serves."[12] The ADA has more than 124,000 members, all of whom also belong to a state society and one of the more than 480 county or city dental societies. The House of Delegates of the ADA, composed of representatives from the constituent state societies, is the "supreme authoritative body of the Association and possesses its legislative powers." It determines policy, approves the

---

[12]Material adapted from *The American Dental Association: Its Structure and Function* (Chicago: American Dental Association, 1975).

annual budget, and elects members of the Board of Trustees of the Association, among other functions. The Board of Trustees holds the administrative authority of the Association and "has the power to conduct all business activities of the Association, to establish rules and regulations to govern Association procedures, to direct production and distribution of the Association's publications and to supervise financial affairs ... appoints the appointive officers ... prepares the annual budget ... (and has the power to) establish *ad interim* policy when the House of Delegates is not in session, provided such policies are later presented for review to the Delegates." Figure 1–12 is an organization chart of the ADA.

Consumers

Perhaps the largest, and least organized, component of the health care system are those people who consume its services. Potentially at least, the ultimate consumers of health care services include everyone in the United States. In reality, not all consumers have equal access to health care services nor do they utilize services in the same way. The experiences with the health care system and the opinions about it are almost as diverse as the U.S. population itself. The results of a major survey of nearly 8,000 people bear this out:

1. A greater percentage of rural Southern blacks can identify a regular source of health care than can urban blacks.
2. Rural farm dwellers are less likely than city residents to see a physician.
3. Among all ethnic groups, low-income Spanish-heritage persons are least likely to see a physician.
4. Blacks spend more time in physicians' waiting rooms than do whites.
5. Members of disadvantaged minorities see physicians less often than do the affluent, but once they start receiving health care, they're apt to seek it more often than the well-to-do.
6. City residents use specialists more frequently than other groups do.
7. Farmers and rural residents make the greatest use of family and general practitioners.
8. More than 6 of every 10 people can get an appointment to see a physician within 2 days, but 8% of the population has to wait more than 2 weeks.
9. Older people are more satisfied with treatment received.
10. People living in the South are least satisfied.
11. People with higher incomes and more education are the most satisfied.
12. Blacks are less satisfied than whites.

30

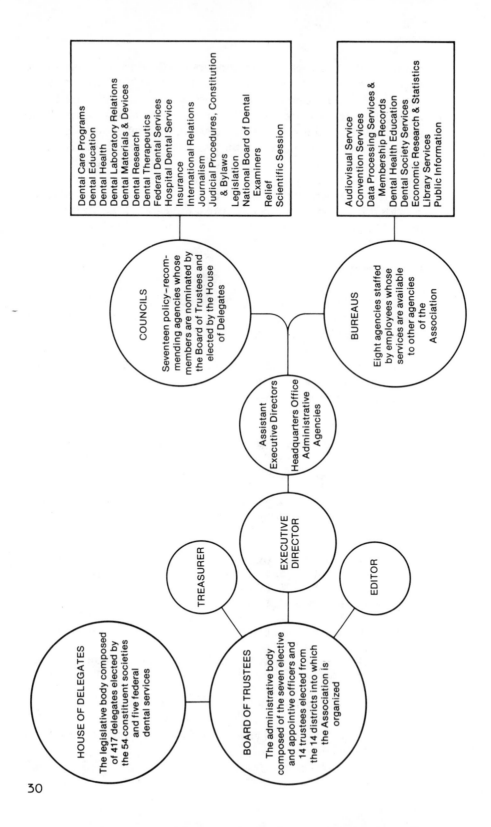

Figure 1–12. Organization of the American Dental Association.

SOURCE: *The American Dental Association: Its Structure and Function* (Chicago: American Dental Association, 1975). p. 9.

13. People who see one physician regularly are more satisfied than those who see a number of physicians.
14. Of all groups, rural Southern blacks are least satisfied.
15. People of Spanish heritage living in the Southwest are less satisfied than are other whites.[13]

On the whole, consumers are remarkably satisfied with the *quality* of health care they receive—80% of Americans express satisfaction with the health care they receive. At the same time, 70% of Americans believe that health care costs are going up too fast and are dissatisfied with this trend.[14] Demand for a larger voice in the decision-making processes that exist in the health care system (a phenomenon termed "consumerism") has never been stronger than today.

Perhaps the most obvious reason for the paucity of active participation in the health care system by consumers, except of course as consumers, is the difficulty any individual faces in relating to large complex systems. (What impact does an individual citizen have on the steel industry, for example?) Although critical questions remain about the knowledgeability and relative persuasive strength of consumers, few seriously question that the consumer, who directly or indirectly pays for the services provided by the health care system, is any longer willing to leave the decision-making power in the health care system entirely in the hands of the other components of the system.

PROBLEMS CONFRONTING THE HEALTH CARE SYSTEM

The health care system faces a dizzying array of problems. The more complex of these problems are not transitory and will not be solved soon or easily. Full enumeration of the set of problems is not possible, for the set developed by one individual or group will differ, frequently in content and almost always in priority, from those developed by someone else. There are even those, although their number has diminished to a naive few, who claim there are no serious problems.

One of the most encouraging signs that the health care system can resolve many of its problems, and perhaps the single

---

[13]Results are from a survey conducted in 1975-1976 by National Opinion Research Center at the University of Chicago as reported in *American Medical News,* January 23, 1978, p. 12.

[14]Health Insurance Association of America, *Health and Health Insurance: the Public's View* (Washington: Health Insurance Association of America, 1983).

greatest strength of the system, is that central components of the system spend considerable energy in identification of its problems. For example, one of the most comprehensive examinations of problems confronting the health care system today has come from a symposium of leading experts convened by the American Hospital Association with support from the National Center for Health Services Research. A book reporting the deliberations of this symposium and summarizing its results sets forth the following set of questions (problems) that face the U.S. health care system.

1. *Cost.* How should society establish means for determining limits on the quantity of resources to be expended on health care services?
2. *Entitlement.* How should society establish a guaranteed minimum set of health care services available for all citizens?
3. *Technology.* How should society establish methods for evaluating the development and use of new medical technologies?
4. *Decision Making.* How should society achieve better decision-making capability by individuals who are not providers of health care services in matters concerning the appropriate allocation, distribution, and use of these services?
5. *Structure.* How should society exert substantial pressures for the reorganization and restructuring of the health care, education, financing, and delivery system to make it more efficient, effective, or economical?[15]

The premier position of cost-concerns reflects the staggering level of total health care expenditures and the steep increases in those expenditures in recent years. But, the other problems are important as well. This set of problems serves to demonstrate the complexity, breadth, and interrelatedness of problems facing the health care system. They will probably be solved in the years ahead because they are such important problems; but as solutions emerge, we can be sure that other equally thorny and important problems will replace them. That is the price of society's effort to achieve a goal so important and so elusive as "complete physical, mental, and social well-being."

SUMMARY

Increasingly, health services are being delivered in a wide variety of organizational settings. At a time when medical knowledge and

---

[15]Donald F. Phillips, "The Public Policy Issues Facing Hospitals in the 1980's," in *Hospitals in the 1980's* (Chicago: American Hospital Association, 1977), pp. 215-234.

clinical capability are at an all-time high, there is a growing dissatisfaction with health services delivery. This reflects the fact that the organization and management of the means of delivering health services have not kept pace with clinical advances. Since so many aspects of the health services organizations described in this chapter are managed by health professionals, it is imperative that they develop management skills. The remainder of the book will deal with the practice of management in the health services organizations in which so many health professionals find themselves. Although we will concentrate on organizations that provide health services, many of the practices described are also applicable to the other types of organizations that comprise the health care system.

The Practice of Management

TWO

APRIL 12TH
9:40 A.M.
The Hospital Administrator's brow furrowed more deeply than usual as he read the letter from the Attorney for Mrs. Luther J. Fillerey. When he had finished the letter, he let it drop to his desk and swiveled his chair around to face the window. Clasping his hands tightly behind his head he rocked the chair back and stared out the window at the grounds of Memorial Hospital.

He had known the letter was coming, and he was not surprised that it requested access to certain hospital records in preparation for the suit the Attorney was preparing.

His mind was cluttered with thoughts:

"How could Luther Fillerey, a young and healthy man, come into this hospital for a bit of routine surgery and develop an infection serious enough to kill him?"

"If we are at fault, how much is this going to cost Memorial, and what effect will it have on our already astronomical malpractice insurance premiums?"

"I never even saw Luther J. Fillerey while he was a patient here and yet, as the manager of this hospital, I must bear the burden for whatever went wrong in our treatment of him."

"It's too bad when a young man, in the prime of his life, is taken away from his family."

"I wish I knew what went wrong; the Board of Trustees will want to know."

"We do our best to set up an organization that can deliver good medical care to everyone who comes here seeking it, but sometimes things just don't work out the way we planned."

"I had better try to find out what went wrong this time."

As he made himself a note to tell the Medical Records Administrator to get Luther Fillerey's medical record in good order, he thought to himself, "Sometimes I wish I managed a factory making televisions. The mistakes could be replaced—nobody can replace Luther J. Fillerey."

At 9:50 a.m., the Administrator picked up some papers from the corner of his desk and hurried off to a Budget Committee meeting.

INTRODUCTION

Many aspects of health organizations are managed by health professionals. The physician who finds himself, as chief of staff, in charge of and responsible for many activities of several hundred fellow physicians needs management skills; the physician in charge of a laboratory or a radiology department needs management skills; the nurse, who as director of nursing is responsible for the largest department in the typical health services organization, must be an effective manager; the head nurse, directly responsible for supervising the nursing care of a group of patients, needs management skills; the pharmacist who is responsible for a critical area of the health services organization needs management skills; the medical social worker's effectiveness can be greatly increased by the proper practice of management; medical or radiologic technologists in charge of a major department need management skills; the physical or respiratory therapist in charge of the department is a manager; the list could go on and on. The point is that, in many cases, the health professional is also a manager in a health services organization.

Setting objectives is a natural human endeavor—to set them in a rational way and to set them for other people requires management skill. To take action is a normal human activity—but action can be more effective and efficient if management skill is exercised, especially when other people are involved in that action. Thus, management is in many ways merely an extension of certain rather routine components of human life. Yet, to manage effectively is a very great challenge indeed! This chapter is about the nature of that challenge and the science (much of which has been codified in a set of principles) that has grown up around it. It is an *overview* of the things one must do to manage successfully. Other chapters in this book treat the topics in more detail. The purpose here is to set out a framework for understanding the challenge of management and to provide a mechanism for viewing the process of management as a coherent, integrated whole.

Although management is an extension of certain rather common human activities, it is a complex extension. There is no widely agreed upon set of principles that can be applied rigidly to every situation. There is not even a universally accepted definition of the management process. Management is not an exact science. Researchers and managers have come to realize in the past few years that the search for universal principles of management is a frustrating one. Sweeping, generalized principles cannot be developed because what works in one setting may not work in another. This phenomenon has been termed the contingency approach to management. The contingency approach suggests that the selection of management practices that should be applied to a given set of circumstances and the manner in which they should be applied are *contingent upon* the particular situation at hand.

This means that, because health services organizations are in many ways unique, management principles and practices should be chosen to be consistent with that uniqueness. For example, health services organizations have a number of features that should influence the approach taken to managing them. Among these features are: the absolute necessity for a high level of quality in the work performed; a very high technology base; the utilization of a wide range of human resources—a range that runs from some of society's most highly trained professionals and scientists to floor washers; the co-existence of automated and manual work methods; and so on. We shall take the contingency approach in this chapter by defining management in terms of the health services organization and by providing an overview of principles of management that are particularly appropriate for situations confronting the manager in that setting.

MANAGEMENT: THE SCIENCE AND THE ART

Management is an art, with a scientific base. "Management as a science can be learned through the study of basic rules, principles, and formulas, but as an art it is often acquired through trial-and-error and years of experience."[1]

Like so many complex concepts, management means different things to different people. As a result, one may find many definitions of the term "management." A common thread in most of these is that when studying management as an academic discipline, or when discussing its relationship to a real work situation, it

---

[1]Richard M. Hodgetts and Dorothy M. Cascio, *Modern Health Care Administration* (New York: Academic Press, 1983), p. 27.

is necessary to think of management as a process. Since a process can be thought of simply as a series of actions directed to some end, we can, by thinking of management as a process, examine in some detail the actions, or functions, which comprise it.

As a beginning point, we will define management as follows: *Management is a process, with both interpersonal and technical aspects, through which the objectives of the health services organization are specified and accomplished by utilizing human and physical resources and technology.* This process can be viewed as a simple input-output relationship in which inputs (human and physical resources and technology) are transformed into desired outputs (accomplishment of the objectives of the organization or some part of it). See Figure 2–1.

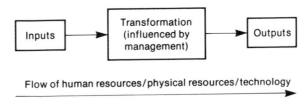

Figure 2–1.   Input-output relationship.

Thus the manager is concerned with achieving objectives and, as we shall see, with first setting objectives. The effective manager is many things—a practical historian learning from the past successes and failures; a psychologist who must understand the way people act in and react to group situations; a theoretician who can develop new ways to achieve desired objectives and apply them in a manner contingent upon the situation at hand. The manager in the health services organization must do two essential things to manage: specify objectives and then see that they are accomplished. The scope of managerial work "includes acquiring and deploying resources, monitoring and interacting with elements in the environment, and facilitating the performance of work"[2] done by a vast array of other people.

THE WORK OF MANAGERS: FUNCTIONS, SKILLS, ROLES

It is possible to take several approaches to an explanation of the work of managers. In this section, three basic approaches—functions, skills, and roles—are described.

---

[2]Martin P. Charns and Marguerite J. Schaefer, *Health Care Organizations: A Model for Management* (Englewood Cliffs, NJ: Prentice-Hall, Inc., 1983), p. 11.

The Functions That Comprise the Management Process

In the practice of management, the manager must take a number of actions. One way to examine the work of the manager is to group these activities into basic categories. Although different authorities categorize these actions in different ways, they may be conveniently viewed as follows: *planning*, which involves the determination of objectives; *organizing*, which is the structuring of people and things to accomplish the work required to fulfill the objectives; *directing*, which is the stimulation of members of the organization toward meeting the objectives; *coordinating*, which is the conscious effort of assembling and synchronizing diverse activities and participants so that they work harmoniously toward the attainment of objectives; and *controlling*, in which the manager compares actual results with objectives to provide a measure of success or failure.

These actions (planning, organizing, directing, coordinating, and controlling) are usually referred to in the management literature as the *functions* of the management process. Perhaps a word of caution is in order here. In discussing the process of management it is convenient, indeed necessary, to separate the functions. So it may seem that the management process is a series of separate functions to be treated as discrete components of the whole. This is not the case at all. In practice, a manager performs each of these functions simultaneously and as part of a continuum. This can be visualized by referring to Figure 2–2. Thus, the

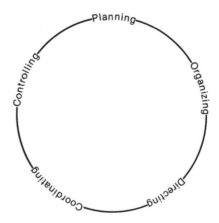

Figure 2–2. The management functions as a continuum.

separation of the management functions is necessary for purposes of discussion, but it is an artificial treatment of the reality of the management process. It does permit us, however, to examine some of the principles that have emerged as to how the various functions should be carried out.

Skills Needed in the Practice of Management

Another way to examine the work of managers is to think about the skills that an effective manager must utilize. Katz has identified three types of skills:[3]

1. *Technical skill* is the ability to use the methods, processes, and techniques of a particular field. It is easy to visualize the technical skills of a surgeon or a physical therapist, but in a similar way, counseling a subordinate or making out a departmental budget also requires a considerable amount of technical skill.

2. *Human skill* is the ability to get along with other people, to understand them, and to motivate and lead them in the work place.

3. *Conceptual skill* is the mental ability to visualize all the complex interrelationships that exist in a work place—interrelationships among people, among departments or units of an organization, and even among a single organization and the environment in which it exists. Conceptual skill permits the manager to understand how the various factors in a particular situation fit together and impact on each other.

Katz suggests that not all managers will need to utilize these skills to the same degree although every manager must rely on all three types of skills in performing his or her work. For example, if one examines the managerial work that goes on in a hospital nursing service, one would find that the director of nursing must rely heavily on conceptual skill because the director is vitally concerned about how nursing service fits into the total picture of the hospital's operation. However, the director can rely on staff them into interpersonal relationships where they must play such

---

[3]Robert L. Katz, "Skills of an Effective Administrator," *Harvard Business Review*, September-October 1974, pp. 90-100.

specialists to take care of much of the technical work. In contrast, a nursing supervisor whose main function is to "trouble-shoot" an entire nursing staff on one shift in the hospital may be constantly required to make decisions on the basis of technical knowledge of nursing while rarely having time to think about the relationship of nursing service to other hospital departments. A head nurse may need a considerable amount of technical skill because in addition to being a manager, this individual also must practice nursing. The head nurse may also, however, be required to exhibit greater human skill on the job than either the director or nursing supervisor since almost all of the head nurse's work involves direct contact with other human beings. This variation in the degree of utilization of these three types of skills may be visualized in Figure 2–3.

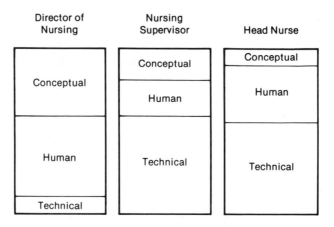

Figure 2–3. Relative skills needed for effective managerial performance in nursing service.

Roles Played by Managers

A third way to examine the work of managers is to think about the different roles they play. Mintzberg has defined roles as "organized sets of behavior" and compared managerial roles to those of actors on a stage. Just as the actor plays a role, the manager, simply because he is a manager, must adopt certain patterns of behavior when he assumes a managerial position.[4] Mintzberg argues that all managers share the common bond of formal authority over the organizational units they manage and that this authority leads

[4]Henry Mintzberg, "The Manager's Job: Folklore and Fact," *Harvard Business Review,* July-August 1975, pp. 49-61.

interpersonal roles as figurehead, leader, and liaison with other units of the organization. These interpersonal roles provide the manager with the opportunity to gather information. This fact, along with what the manager does with the information, permits a second set of roles. These *informational roles* include monitor, disseminator, and spokesman roles. Finally, the authority granted to managers, supported by their interpersonal and informational roles, requires that they play *decisional roles*. These include disturbance handler, resource allocator, and negotiator roles. In addition, a key decisional role for every manager is that of entrepreneur in which the manager functions as an initiator and designer of changes intended to improve the unit over which he or she has authority. These ten managerial roles are summarized in Figure 2–4. Mintzberg has pointed out that these roles cannot be

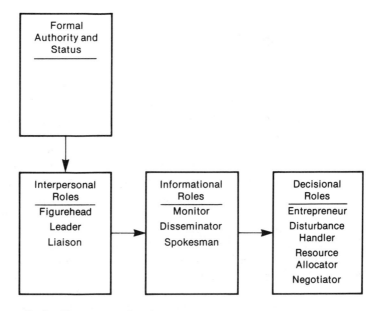

Figure 2–4. The manager's roles.

SOURCE: Henry Mintzberg, "The Manager's Job: Folklore and Fact," *Harvard Business Review,* July-August 1975, p. 55. Copyright © 1975 by the President and Fellows of Harvard College; all rights reserved.

separated. "They are tightly linked together in what the psychologist would call a gestalt, an integrated whole. The manager's job is not simply the algebraic sum of these ten roles, but much more— the whole that results when these roles are linked together in the managerial job."[5]

[5] Jay W. Lorsch, James P. Baughman, James Reece, and Henry Mintzberg, *Understanding Management* (New York: Harper & Row Publishers, 1978), p. 221.

We can see that the work of managers can be viewed from three perspectives: the functions they perform, the skills they need, and the roles they play. In the remaining chapters of this book, we will integrate all three viewpoints. However, for purposes of providing a framework for the book, we will take a functional approach. That is, we will examine the functions of planning, organizing, directing, coordinating, and controlling as they are carried out by the manager in the health services organization. In the remaining sections of this chapter, we will describe each of these functions briefly and look at some of the special aspects of practicing management in the health services organization.

THE MANAGERIAL FUNCTIONS BRIEFLY DESCRIBED

Planning

The primary management function is *planning*. In essence, planning means to decide in advance what is to be done. It charts a course of action for the future. The aim of planning is to achieve a coordinated and consistent set of operations aimed at desired objectives. Without planning, random activities prevail. Planning is basically an intellectual process and as such is easy or difficult for individuals depending upon their capacities. It is so basic to management that planning must be done by all managers whether they find it easy or not. Logically, planning is the first of the management functions. It lays the foundation for organizing—an organization structure is designed to help carry out plans. It dictates those activities to which employees are directed. It facilitates coordination. Finally, during the planning activity, standards are set against which actual performance can be measured when management carries out the control function. As conditions change, plans have to be constantly revised and updated. It is a continuous activity for management. While planning can be discussed as a separate function of management, it must be remembered that it intertwines and overlaps with the other managerial functions. There is no clearcut sequence of functions that managers perform one after another.

A number of reasons, outlined below, explain why planning is so critically important in today's health services organizations.

1. *To focus attention on objectives.* Good planning yields reasonable organizational objectives and develops alternative approaches to meeting these objectives. In this way planning

provides a means of unifying the actions of all organizational participants toward common ends. Health services organizations of all kinds are undergoing a serious reevaluation, both internally and in the eyes of many interested parties external to the organizations, in terms of their roles in health delivery and the manner in which they operate. Planning is the function that allows organizations to decide where they should be going and literally forces a determination of the means to get there.

2. *To offset uncertainty and chance.* The only thing certain about the future is uncertainty. No one knows what changes will occur even one day in advance. The further into the future one looks, the less the certainty. However, if the manager thinks about the future and plans for those contingencies he can imagine or foresee, he will greatly reduce the chance of being caught unprepared. He cannot eliminate uncertainty or chance, but he can prepare for it through planning. The means of delivering health services to the population of this country are undergoing significant changes. These changes require that the organizations that deliver these services be adaptable and flexible.

3. *To gain economical operation.* The costs of health services, particularly those provided in organized settings, are rising at a very fast rate. While many aspects of cost are beyond the manager's control, some can be minimized through planning for efficient operation and consistency. Planning substitutes integrated effort for random activity, controlled flow of work for uneven flow, and careful decisions for snap judgments. As the delivery of health services becomes more and more an organizational effort, the managerial function of planning becomes increasingly important as a means of controlling service costs.

4. *To facilitate control.* Control implies comparing actual results with some predetermined desired result. The planning function yields information that can be used to set standards against which actual results can be compared. As third parties, principally the government through Medicare and Medicaid, have assumed a greater share of the health care financial burden, they have required significantly more accountability from health services providers. This accountability goes beyond cost to include both the quality of care and the manner in which it is delivered. The trend toward more accountability and the concurrent necessity for control that it implies will become increasingly important in health services

organizations in the years ahead. From the manager's perspective, the effect of planning on the effort to control those
activities for which he or she is responsible is one of the most
important reasons for effective planning.

Organizing

Once objectives have been established through planning, management concern must turn to developing an organization that is
capable of carrying them out. The basic objective of the *organizing*
function is development of a structure or framework called the
formal organization structure. Organizing can be defined as relating people and things to each other in such a way that they are
combined into a unit capable of being directed toward organization
objectives. The most basic premise of organization is that division
of work is essential for efficiency. Work activities required for
organizational performance are separated through the process of
vertical and horizontal differentiation (i.e., dividing the organization into operational units). Vertical differentiation establishes the
hierarchy and the number of levels in the organization. Horizontal
differentiation comes about because of the need to separate
activities for more effective and efficient performance. This usually
results in the formation of departments within the organization.

The formal organization depends on two basic relationships:
(1) responsibility and (2) authority. Responsibility can be thought of
as the obligation to execute functions of work. The source of
responsibility is one's superior in the organization. By delegating
responsibility to a subordinate, the superior creates a relationship
based on obligation between himself and the subordinate. The
basis for dividing responsibility in organizations is functional
similarity. The total work load of an organization is divided among
available personnel by grouping functions that are similar in
objectives and content. This should be done in a manner that
avoids overlaps and gaps as much as possible. Responsibility may
be continuing or it may be terminated by the accomplishment of a
single action.

When responsibility is given to a person, he must also be
given the authority to make commitments, use resources, and take
the actions necessary to carry out his responsibilities. Authority
and responsibility must be commensurate. If authority exceeds
responsibility, a misuse of authority can occur. Conversely, a
person who is delegated responsibility without adequate authority
to fulfill it finds it to be a most frustrating and often embarrassing
position. The tangible product of the delegation of authority and
responsibility is a formal organization structure.

Directing

Once plans have been made and an organization has been created to put them into effect, the next logical function of management is to stimulate the effort needed to perform the required work. This is done through the directing function, which includes the following activities:

1. Order giving
2. Supervising
3. Leading
4. Motivating
5. Communicating

No matter what approach one takes to management, at some point the manager has to indicate what he or she wants done. The order is the technical means through which a subordinate understands what is to be done.

Supervision is the activity of management that is concerned with the training and discipline of the work force. It includes follow-up to ensure the prompt and proper execution of orders. In this sense it is also a part of the control function, which will be discussed later. Supervising is a required function for every manager from the top of the health services organization on down.

Leadership is the ability to inspire and influence others to contribute to the attainment of objectives. It is obviously necessary for getting work done through and by others—which is the manager's task. Traditionally, success in leadership was thought to be dependent on traits of the leader. More recently, it has been shown that successful leadership is the result of interaction between the leader and his or her subordinates in a particular organizational situation. This means that a single pattern of leadership behavior used without discretion is not likely to be successful in a wide variety of managerial situations. Thus, the successful leader is not a blind follower of particular leadership methods but chooses the method that he or she considers most appropriate for a given situation. The leader reaches a choice by considering the overall situation, especially the subordinates, and what effect his or her actions will have on them.

The manager must always keep in mind that getting an employee to carry out a directive is *caused* behavior. In that sense, the manager must motivate, or cause, the employee to follow directives. The importance of motivation skill for the manager cannot be overemphasized. There is a growing body of sound

empirical evidence that the best motivator is a challenging job—
one that allows a feeling of achievement, responsibility, growth,
advancement, enjoyment of the work itself, and earned recognition. This is especially true with professional and high-skill-level
workers. Jobs that have these characteristics do not just happen.
They must be created by, and carefully nurtured by, the manager.

Communicating with workers is the final activity of the effort
to direct their work performance. In a sense it is the key to directing
because unless a manager can effectively communicate what is to
be done, how it is to be done, by whom it is to be done, and why it
is to be done, the chances of adequately carrying out the directing
function are greatly reduced.

Communication in highly complex organizations such as
those providing health services is a multidirectional process requiring movement downward, upward, and in all directions necessary
to reach associates and peer-level positions. It is a process of
people relating to each other. As they do so in performing work and
solving problems, they communicate facts, ideas, feelings, and
attitudes. If this communication is effective, the work gets done
more effectively and the problems are solved more efficiently.

Coordinating

Coordinating is the act of synchronizing people and activities so
that they function smoothly in the attainment of organization
objectives. The importance of this managerial function cannot be
overemphasized. Fulmer has said, "It is the closest thing to a
synonym that we could find for management."[6] Koontz, O'Donnell,
and Weihrich have also said, "It becomes the central task of the
manager to reconcile differences in approach, timing, effort, or
interest and to harmonize cooperative and individual goals."[7]

Different kinds of organizations require different amounts of
coordination. In some organizations it is possible to separate
activities in such a way as to minimize these requirements. In other
organizations, particularly those such as health services organizations, which are departmentalized functionally, coordination is
more important. One must recognize the interaction between the
need to specialize activities and the requirements for coordination.
The more differentiation of activities and specialization of labor, the
more difficult are the problems of coordination. Hospitals, for

[6]Robert M. Fulmer, *The New Management* (New York: Macmillan Publishing Company, Inc., 1974), p. 84.

[7]Harold Koontz, Cyril O'Donnell and Heinz Weihrich, *Management* (New York:
McGraw-Hill Book Company, 1980), p. 82.

example, are among the most complex organizations in modern society in terms of differentiation of activities and specialization of labor. They are characterized by a detailed division of labor into a number of technical skills. The work of the institution is so specialized and performed by such a variety of workers that very significant problems of coordination often arise. Furthermore, in the hospital, organizational activities are often contingent on one another. It is this condition of functional interdependence among organizational parts and activities that make coordination so important in hospitals.

Many authorities see that the essential challenge of coordination stems from the fact that individuals often perceive objectives differently and also lean toward varying methods of accomplishing those objectives. This means that coordinating, in a very real sense, means managing conflict. Conflict may be between various functional groups in the health services organization, such as between the medical staff and administration, or between nursing service and the laboratory. But it may also be conflict between subordinate and superior, between the individual and the organization, or between two peers. Any one of these and other relationships is a potential source of conflict. As we shall see later, not all conflict is bad, but even such low levels of conflict as are evidenced by "disliking" and "difficulty in getting along with" are often associated with reduced effectiveness. In essence, coordination is a preventive managerial function concerned with heading off conflict and misunderstanding.

Controlling

Controlling can be defined as the regulation of activities in accordance with the requirements of plans. By definition, control is directly linked to the planning function. This may be stated in another way: the managerial function of control consists of measuring and correcting activities of people and things in an organization to ensure that objectives and plans are accomplished. It is a function of all managers on all levels, and its basic purpose is to ensure that what is intended to be done is what is done. Control techniques are based upon the same basic elements regardless of whether people, quality of care, money, or morale is being controlled. The control process, wherever it is applied, involves four steps: (1) establishing standards, (2) measuring performance, (3) comparing actual results with standards, and (4) correcting deviations from standards.

THE PRACTICE OF MANAGEMENT

THE NEED FOR MANAGEMENT OF HEALTH PROFESSIONALS

Provision of high quality health services is the basic objective of health professionals. Determination of the need for, and the development of, organizations that can provide these services would be a formidable management task even without the constraints of scarce resources. However, given these constraints and the fact that consumers must expend an increasingly large portion of their incomes on health services, another objective has become important in the operation of health services organizations. That is the responsibility to provide needed services of high quality *in the most efficient way possible*. Health services organizations must now be concerned not only with the scope and quality of their services but also the efficiency with which these services are provided. The dual concern for quality and efficiency places a tremendous burden on health professionals and those who manage them. Yet it is a burden they must bear if the nation is to have high quality health care that is both available and affordable.

The manager in the health services organization must be concerned with both quality and productivity at the same time. He or she cannot emphasize one to the detriment of the other. Figure 2–5 illustrates this. The diagram shows that the (1, 1) manager would have low concern for both quality and productivity in providing health services. Hopefully, this is a hypothetical case. The (10, 1) manager would be highly concerned with quality but would lose his effectiveness because he is unconcerned about productivity. A health services organization can tolerate some managers of this type (many of them do), but if everyone were this way, the organization in all likelihood could not function in today's atmosphere of economic constraints. The (1, 10) position is not desirable because, although a manager who takes this approach is concerned about productivity, this type of individual has a low concern for quality— an intolerable position for one who provides vital health services. The (5, 5) position indicates a median but balanced concern for both quality and productivity. It is a desirable position from the perspective of its balance but undesirable in that it represents a half-hearted concern for both quality and productivity. It is a "getting by" position and, as such, does not represent a best effort toward which everyone should strive. The (10, 10) position—maximum concern for both quality and productivity—may also be hypothetical, given the nature of human effort, but it is clearly the most desirable position for a manager to occupy. There are, of course, a limitless number of other managerial positions on this

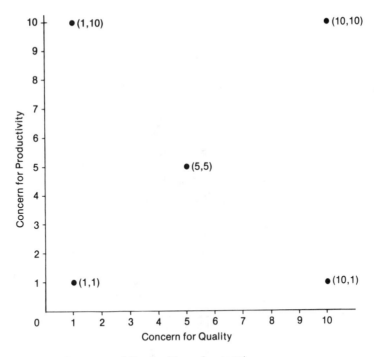

Figure 2–5. Concerns of the health professional.

diagram. The point is that the manager should strive for the (10,10) position to maximize effectiveness.

It has frequently been argued that the quality of health services is a basic determinant of the cost of delivering health services. Clearly, severe attempts to curtail costs could reduce quality of care if they resulted in inadequate staffing or lack of certain necessary equipment and supplies. Of more practical interest, however, is the relationship between quality and costs that does not represent extremes. In a study conducted by the author using four measures of quality and two measures of productivity, it was found that hospitals able to provide services in an efficient manner tend to produce services of higher quality than those that operate less efficiently (where direct costs are higher). This suggests that the ideal objective of high quality services at the lowest possible cost is not only desirable but pragmatic and consistent. The two go hand in hand and are strongly influenced by effective management.[8]

---

[8]Beaufort B. Longest, Jr., "Hospital Services: An Empirical Analysis of Their Quality-Cost Relationship," *Hospital and Health Services Administration,* Fall 1978, pp. 20-35.

Quality and Quantity

The manager of health professionals has to be concerned with both quality and quantity of work. The quality aspect derives largely from the professional training these people receive and, therefore, will not be treated at length in this book. The reader is reminded that this book is intended to fill in the "management gaps" that many health professionals have. The bulk of our effort will be to offer methods by which productivity (the quantity of work) can be improved. However, when we discuss the controlling function of management (Chapter 9), we shall look at the problems associated with controlling the quality of health services.

Productivity is, in and of itself, a very complex concept. It is affected by a number of factors. Figure 2–6 illustrates the interrela-

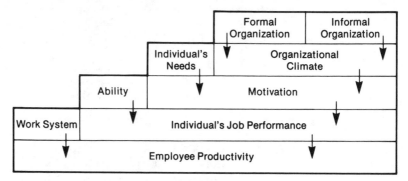

Figure 2–6. Employee productivity. (Appreciation is expressed to Professor Jonathan S. Rakich of the University of Akron for his help in this conceptualization.)

tionships of factors affecting employee productivity.[9] We shall describe them briefly here and then in more depth in subsequent chapters. Employee productivity is directly influenced by the individual's job performance and the work system (the technical arrangements and facilities for work). The individual's job performance is directly affected by his or her ability (innate and learned abilities) and motivation. The motivation of the individual is directly affected by individual needs and the organizational climate (total environmental context in which the individual works) as it permits or prohibits him or her from fulfilling needs. The organizational climate is, in turn, influenced by both the formal and informal aspects of the organization.

---

[9]A much more comprehensive set of factors can be seen in Robert A. Sutermeister, *People and Productivity* (New York: McGraw-Hill Book Company, 1976).

SPECIAL CHARACTERISTICS OF HEALTH PROFESSIONALS

The basic contribution of health professionals is intellectual in nature. They provide knowledge to be used in meeting the objectives of health services organizations. So the problem facing managers in the health care setting is one of integrating management authority and the knowledge brought in by the health professionals.

Etzioni suggests that there are three basic ways in which knowledge is handled in organizations:

1. Knowledge is produced, applied, preserved, or communicated in organizations especially established for these purposes. These are professional organizations, which are characterized not only by the goals they pursue but also by the high proportion of professionals on their staff (at least 50 percent) and by the authority relations between professionals and nonprofessionals which are so structured that professionals have superior authority over the major goal activities of the organization. Professional organizations include universities, colleges, most schools, research organizations, therapeutic mental hospitals, the larger general hospitals, and social-work agencies.

2. There are service organizations in which professionals are provided with the instruments, facilities, and auxiliary staff required for their work. The professionals, however, are not employed by the organization nor subordinate to its administrators. An example would be a research organization attached to a university which has no professional staff of its own but which utilizes members of the faculty and provides them with computers, laboratories, clerical and research assistance, and other means which their work requires.

3. Professionals may be employed by organizations whose goals are nonprofessional, such as industrial and military establishments. Here professionals are often assigned to special divisions or positions, which to one degree or another take into account their special needs. In these organizations the knowledge of the scientist and professional are utilized by the organization as an input to accomplish its goals and objectives. Thus the corporation uses many scientists and professionals to accomplish the major organizational goals. Typically, scientists and professionals are assigned to auxiliary or "staff" units within the organization.[10]

Clearly, most health services organizations are "professional organizations" in the sense that they employ a large number of

---

[10]Amitai Etzioni, *Modern Organizations* (Englewood Cliffs, N.J.: Prentice-Hall, Inc., 1964).

professionals who produce, apply, preserve, and communicate knowledge.

In order to manage these professional human resources, it is necessary first to understand those characteristics that set health care professionals apart from other occupational groups. This is not to say that they are completely different from other members of the work force. They do, however, exhibit certain characteristics to a greater degree than do other people. For example, they have a high need for achievement and self-actualization. They have a keen interest in their work and the development of knowledge for its own sake. They are motivated by problems that have an intrinsic importance to them. They tend to be inner-directed rather than motivated through external rewards or punishments. Another characteristic of health professionals is what Alvin Gouldner calls the differences in cosmopolitan and local orientation. He describes them as follows:

> *Cosmopolitans:* Those low on loyalty to the employing organization, high on commitment to specialized role skills, and likely to use an outer reference group orientation.
>
> *Locals:* Those high on loyalty to the employing organization, low on commitment to specialized role skills, and likely to use an inner reference group orientation.[11]

While there are exceptions, most health professionals tend to be more cosmopolitan than local. The local seeks advancement through the organizational hierarchy and wants recognition from superiors. He generally exhibits less discontent over organizational requirements, responds more to incentives such as hierarchial status, and identifies with the goals, values, and status system of the organization—he is internally oriented. The cosmopolitan, in contrast, is oriented toward his profession. He seeks advancement and status in his profession through approval of colleagues, identifies with the profession's goals, and seeks external recognition. He generally exhibits discontent over organizational requirements that interfere with his work, responds less to organizational incentives than professional incentive, and identifies with the goals, values, and status system of his profession—he is externally oriented.

There is always the danger of creating unwarranted stereotypes in generalizing about any group of people. Clearly, there are many health professionals who do not exhibit the characteristics described above—at least, there are varying degrees of the charac-

----

[11]Alvin W. Gouldner, "Cosmopolitans and Locals: Toward an Analysis of Latent Social Roles, I," *Administrative Science Quarterly,* December 1957, p. 290.

teristics among health professionals. Yet these generalizations are widely applicable and can be helpful to the person who manages health professionals.

CONTINGENCY THEORY AND MANAGING HEALTH PROFESSIONALS

We have described management as a process made up of several functions. The reader, especially one who has been involved in complex health services organizations, no doubt realizes that management is not so simple as performing a set of functions. Perhaps the one thing we can say with complete confidence about management is that there is *no one best way* to organize and manage a health services organization or any part of it. What works best for one group in one setting may not work best for another group in another setting. Several writers have formalized this concept, calling it the Contingency or Situational Theory of Management.[12]

For the manager to impose sameness dictatorially on those he or she manages is not management. The art and the science of the practice of management is to draw out the strengths of those who are managed and to direct them toward the achievement of objectives—by whatever methods that work.

A key point for the manager of health professionals is that effective management is an essential ingredient in the effective delivery of health services. It is no longer desirable or possible to separate clinical and managerial activities in the delivery of health services. As Stephen Shortell has stated:

> Increasingly complex reimbursement schemes, legal decisions, utilization review regulations, and a generally more informed and demanding public (to name but a few factors) have precipitated the integration or, perhaps more accurately, confrontation of the administrative and clinical spheres of influence. Administrative activities increasingly touch upon the practice of medicine, and clinical practice, in turn, is heavily involved with issues of managerial efficiency and effectiveness.[13]

---

[12]See for example, Fremont E. Kast and James E. Rosenzweig, *Organization and Management: A Systems and Contingency Approach* (New York: McGraw-Hill Book Company, 1979).

[13]Stephen M. Shortell, "Hospital Medical Staff Organization: Structure, Process and Outcome," *Hospital Administration*, Spring 1974, p. 105.

With this background on the management process, we are ready to turn our attention to an examination of specific aspects of the management functions—especially as they apply to the management of health professionals.

SUMMARY

The art and science of the practice of management is a process, with both interpersonal and technical aspects, through which the objectives of an organization, or that part of it being managed, are established and accomplished by utilizing human and physical resources and technology. The functions of management (planning, organizing, directing, coordinating, and controlling) have been briefly described. The need for management of health professionals in today's organizational setting has been emphasized. We have described the dual responsibility of health professionals to provide needed services of high quality but in an efficient manner. Attention has also been given to some of the special characteristics of health professionals.

Planning: The Beginning of Management

THREE

"Will the meeting come to order?" the Hospital Administrator asked. "We have a long agenda." The fourteen Department Heads for Memorial Hospital settled into their seats around the conference table anticipating another lengthy round of Planning Committee deliberations.

Before anyone else could speak, the Medical Records Administrator cleared her throat and spoke, "Listen, while we're all together I'd like to ask that everyone have all the documentation on the treatment of Mr. Luther J. Fillerey, patient number 3222-004, forwarded to Medical Records if you haven't already done so. As you may know, his family is bringing suit against the hospital, and I have to get his medical record in good order."

The Director of Nursing asked, "What's missing? He died over two months ago!"

The Medical Records Administrator responded, "Some of the lab reports are not in, and I'm pretty sure that there is some radiology work that is not yet in the record." Her voice reflected irritation as she added, "And some of the nurses' notes haven't been signed."

The Hospital Administrator leaned forward in his chair and interrupted by saying, "I know how important this suit is to all of us, and I know that it is upsetting...but this meeting is supposed to be devoted to long-range planning for the hospital; not these day-to-day problems." He slumped back and looked at the ceiling as he continued, "This Planning Committee meets once a month for the purpose of setting long-range planning recommendations that I can pass on to the Board of Trustees. Yet, every month we have a new crisis on our hands, and we end up devoting the meeting to it. Last month it was our accreditation site visit, this month it's the suit...who knows what it will be next month." The Department Heads sat motionless and silent as the Administrator admonished them, "If we always spend our time fighting fires, we'll never get around to long-range planning!"

The Director of the Social Service Department used a pause in the Administrator's speech to exclaim, "The most important thing facing Memorial Hospital is this suit. It affects everything from patient confidence in us to the financial stability of the hospital."

The Controller supported her view, "This suit is for a million dollars. If we lose it, our insurance premiums are going to go through the ceiling!"

For the next hour and twenty minutes, the topic never varied from the suit brought against the hospital by the family of Luther J. Fillerey.

The meeting adjourned at 2:40 p.m.

INTRODUCTION

Health services organizations operate in an environment of change. They must be able and prepared to accept change as the inevitable consequence of operating in a dynamic world. The general political, social, economic, and technological environment in which health services are delivered means that continued success and further development demands adaptation and innovation. In such an environment, effective planning ability is a necessary tool for the effective manager.

The modern health services organization faces a future that no one can predict with certainty. Effective planning can reduce the impact of this uncertainty. Internally, managers must plan for means of solving the problems of procurement, allocation, and utilization of resources; striking the balance between formal and informal organizational patterns; coordinating diverse but interdependent efforts; developing suitable reward and incentive programs; integrating organizational requirements with the needs and goals of participants; developing suitable leadership and supervisory skills at all levels of the organization; and anticipating all of the other "internal" problems faced by health services managers.

On the other hand, managers must plan for appropriate responses to the set of problems stemming from the "external" relationships of the organization, to the needs and demands of the community it serves, and to other relevant outside groups that have an interest in the organization. The viability and effectiveness of the health services organization depend upon the ability of its managers to plan for the impact of these and other factors on the organization.

PLANNING DEFINED

Planning can be defined as deciding in advance what is to be done and how it is to be done. The "what" decisions lead to the establishment of objectives, and the "how" decisions lead to the determination of methods for achieving those objectives.

59

Planning is done on many levels in the health care field. For example, what has come to be called "comprehensive," or "area-wide," planning deals with the interrelationships of various health providers in a given area—e.g., a hospital that participates in area-wide planning may decide not to develop an open-heart surgery capability if adequate facilities already exist in the area. As we noted in Chapter 1, Health Systems Agencies (HSAs) now have the responsibility for developing area-wide plans for health services and facilities.

Planning is also done at the level of the individual health services organization. The determination of "what is to be done and how it is to be done" at the level of an organization, such as a hospital, results in a statement of objectives (what) and methods (how) for the entire organization. The development of these objectives and methods is the responsibility of top level administrators, although they need the participation of many other people to develop them fully.

Planning is also done at many levels *within* the individual health services organization. The manager of each department or unit of the organization must determine what is to be done and how it is to be done in his unit. We can think of this as the determination of objectives (what) and methods (how) that will guide the actions of those people being managed as well as the use of resources that are available to the manager. While all these levels of planning are important in the overall scheme of health services delivery, we are primarily concerned with the last level—planning within the health services organization at the level of departments or sub-parts. We will focus our attention on the determination of what is to be done (setting objectives) and how it is to be done (developing methods). Before we examine these aspects of planning, however, it will be useful to set the stage by describing planning at the level of the health services organization (at this level, planning is often referred to as strategy formulation) and by describing several key elements that pertain to the management function of planning.

STRATEGY FORMULATION

Strategy is the set of decisions that determine the character (size, scope, and mix of services) of a health services organization and give it direction in the marketplace. From this definition, it is obvious that a great many individual decisions make up the strategy of a particular health services organization at a particular time. However, it is possible to characterize the strategy of a health services organization in general ways such as a "growth strategy" or a "reputation enhancement strategy" or a "stabilization strategy," to mention only a few possibilities.

The strategy of an organization does not simply emerge by chance. It is formulated by people for an organization that exists in relationship to an external environment upon which the organization is highly dependent.[1] Appreciating this external dependency phenomenon is quite important in order to understand what strategy is and how it is formulated. The external dependency relationship between a hospital, for example, and its environment can be outlined as follows:

1. Hospitals find themselves dependent, in varying degrees, on elements (competitors, suppliers, labor markets, consumers, and regulators) in their external environments.

2. Hospital managers, because of this dependence on external environment, must constantly view the external environment as a series of opportunities and/or threats.

3. Those responsible for managing hospitals try to capitalize on the opportunities and defend their organizations against the threats that face them.

4. Managers' efforts to respond to the opportunities and threats from the external environment heavily influence and are directly reflected in the strategy elaborated for the hospital.

Figure 3–1 illustrates the strategy formulation process and shows the relationship between the external environment of the

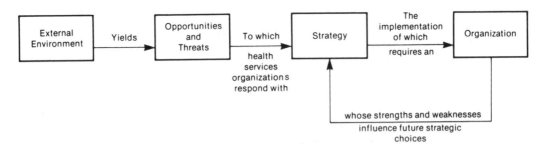

Figure 3–1. The strategy formulation process.

---

[1] For an excellent treatment of the external dependency perspective see: Jeffrey Pfeffer and Gerald R. Salancik, *The External Control of Organizations: A Resource Dependence Perspective* (New York: Harper & Row, Publishers, 1978).

health services organization and the strategy elaborated for it. Mintzberg has suggested that strategy formulation in an organization facing a complex, demanding, and constantly changing environment will be an adaptive process.[2] As Figure 3–1 illustrates, the strategy of a health services organization will be an adaptation by managers to perceived opportunities and threats presented to their organizations by their external environments and influenced by extant strengths and weaknesses of their organization. Longest has demonstrated that the dependence of health services organizations on their external environments is so great that their strategic responses to particular environmental circumstances are largely predictable.[3]

As Lefko has suggested, "strategic planning will form the foundation for those institutions that can effectively manage their resources and their changing internal and external environments."[4] The nature of some of the changes that hospitals can anticipate into the next decade and a look at their past and present environments are reflected in Table 3–1.

KEY ELEMENTS IN THE PLANNING FUNCTION

Any consideration of the basic elements in planning as they relate to management of a health services organization, or any part of it, should center around four points: evaluation of present conditions; the time factor; collection and analysis of data; and a hierarchy of plans within the health services organization.

Evaluation of Present Conditions

Perhaps the central element in the planning function is recognizing in present conditions any inadequacies that require change. Once these undesirable conditions have been identified, the question arises of what to do about them. It is the existence of alternative answers to this question that gives rise to planning. Earlier in this chapter we outlined some of the internal and external problems faced by health services managers. Given the complexities of meeting the health care needs of our citizens today, it would be

[2]Henry Mintzberg, "Strategy-Making in Three Modes," *California Management Review,* Vol. 26 (1973), pp. 44-53.

[3]Beaufort B. Longest, Jr., "An External Dependence Perspective of Organizational Strategy and Structure: The Community Hospital Case," *Hospital and Health Services Administration,* Spring 1981, pp. 50-69.

[4]Jeffrey J. Lefko, "A Portfolio of Progress," *Hospitals,* June 1, 1983, p. 82.

TABLE 3-1. *The Changing Hospital Planning Environment—Past, Present, Future*

Change	1973	1983	1993
"Snapshot" characteri- zation	• Freestanding hospitals providing primarily acute care with growing inpatient demand • Focus on encouraging use of inpatient hospitalization and expanding hospital beds	• Discouragement of inpatient hospital care • Increased competition for a dwindling, stabilized inpatient demand and revenue base • Diversification efforts aimed at seeking out new markets and income sources	• Closed hospital systems selectively determining health niche in an openly competitive, "bottom line" oriented patient market • Inpatient utilization only by those requiring hospitalization; others treated outside hospitals in a variety of noninstitutional settings
Hospital role and mission	• Singular in purpose • Oriented to acute inpatient care • Informally identified	• Plurality of purpose • Oriented to both acute and ambulatory care • Documented and formally identified	• Multidimensional purposes • Multitude of businesses, both hospital- and non-hospital-related • Specifically delineated and enunciated
Hospital link to external environment	• Relatively independent of external environment	• Generally dependent on external environment	• Intimately dependent on external environment
Financial reimburse- ment and structure	• Mounting concern over increasing hospital costs • Commencement of federal regulations to control costs • Retrospective cost- or charge-based reimbursement for hospital services • Sufficient available capital for expansion or renovation • Limited price consideration in purchase of hospital services	• Emphasis on payment system reform to control costs • Reduced federal- and state-sponsored reimbursement of health care services • Limited and expensive capital to fund growth and development • Case-mix orientation • Increasing competition and price sensitivity in marketplace • Declining availability of traditional capital sources	• Provider reimbursement based on institutional competencies, resources, and prices • Federally controlled lid on hospital costs • Use of imaginative and creative payment approaches • Hospital reorganization to allow for limited capital sources • Uniform payment for patient diagnosis
Hospital/ medical staff relationships	• Provision of all necessary institutional resources for medical staff • Close working alignment between hospitals and medical staffs	• Competition between hospitals and physicians to undertake traditional hospital services • New interest in corporate and financial physician/ hospital arrangements	• Corporate grouping of physicians and hospitals • Innovative arrangements involving hospitals, physicians, and investors
National health planning initiatives	• Transition from planning agencies to regulatory agencies • Beginning of CON legislation	• National health planning in state of flux • Shift from federal to state jurisdiction • Continued control of capital expenditures and health resource supply	• Health planning continuing to address community care issues • Federal efforts regulate health resource supply aided by limited capital sources *(continued)*

TABLE 3-1. (Cont.)

Change	1973	1983	1993
New technology	• Rapid implementation of advanced technology	• Reduced implementation of advanced technology • Priorities shift to limited capital resources and increased CON constraints	• Selective implementation of new technology only in tertiary referral centers
Hospital organization and governance	• Dominated by freestanding independent hospitals with autonomous governing boards	• Plethora of multihospital arrangements • Board control increasingly geographically and organizationally separate from institutions	• Freestanding hospitals to be exceptions • Multi-institutional arrangements to be predominant • National megasystems become commonplace • Centralized governance through fewer and more geographically disparate boards
institutional management	• Generalist approach to hospital management • Facility and bed orientation • Knowledge of computer assistance in financial operation	• Multidisciplinary specialist approach to management • Emphasis on strategic and market-based planning • Knowledge of computer application in medical and management information systems	• Required sophisticated and specialized management expertise • Multidisciplinary techniques required for program initiatives • Pressing need for integrating clinical, administrative, and financial decision-making • Need for sophisticated strategic management in hospitals • Knowledge of complex computer-assisted decision-making techniques

SOURCE: Jeffrey J. Lefko, "A Portfolio of Progress," *Hospitals*, Vol. 57, No. 11 (June 1, 1983), pp. 78-82. Reprinted, with permission, from *Hospitals*, published by American Hospital Publishing, Inc., copyright June 1, 1983, Vol. 57, No. 11.

extremely naive of any manager to feel that there is nothing more that could be done to improve the activities for which he or she is responsible.

The Time Factor

The problem of timing of events is very important in planning. Perhaps this is nowhere more apparent than in relation to patient care. Suppose a person is admitted to a hospital, for example, to have a certain surgical procedure performed. Many decisions have to be made about this patient far enough in advance to allow the procedure to go smoothly and provide the patient an opportunity to get maximum benefit from his stay in the hospital. This is known as lead time. Different activities associated with this patient's surgical episode require different amounts of time. If we wish to coordinate events with different lead times, we must analyze the points at which we want coordination to take place and schedule events accordingly. To further complicate this, there is usually a sequence in which events have to take place; hence we must make provision for sequential lead times. The surgical episode is only one example. Indeed, most activities in health services organizations are related to and dependent upon other activities, often in other departments or units, and must be considered in light of this fact.

It is essential to grasp another aspect of the time factor in relation to planning—that short-range and long-range planning are aspects of the same continuous activity. Success in planning depends on the ability of managers to understand that short-range planning can be successful only if it is carried out in the context of adequate long-range planning.

Collection and Analysis of Data

Effective planning depends on the quality and quantity of data available to the manager. Consideration must be given to pertinent data from the present and the past, and an assessment must be made of probable future events. The assessment of probable future events is more than peering into a crystal ball. It is the establishment of assumptions or forecasts of the future that bear upon present actions. For example, how many tests of a certain type are going to be performed by the laboratory in the coming year? How many person-hours will be required? What equipment and supplies will be needed? The answers to these and similar questions will provide the premises upon which planning will take place in the laboratory. Similar premises can be established for other units in the health services organization. The fact that premises cannot be established with certainty makes it essential that plans contain built-in flexibility.

Planning premises include three types of information: estimates of factual data, policies of the organization, and future plans of the organization as a whole. Perhaps examples of each type of premise will help clarify them. To continue with the laboratory example, its manager can estimate that the laboratory will perform 2,000 tests of a certain type. This is an example of an estimate of factual data. An organization policy that should be considered a planning premise for human resources needs is a situation in which the organization has a policy of requiring some minimum level of experience for certain jobs. Another might be a policy of promoting from within wherever possible. An example of the plans of the entire organization serving as a planning premise for a department would be a plan to open a new wing during the next year. This must be taken into account in plans of each department in the health services organization.

Premising is the assessment of the future. For the institution as a whole, and to only a slightly smaller extent for individual departments or units within the organization, it is becoming necessary to forecast further and further into the future.

A Hierarchy of Plans Within the Health Services Organization

It is important to realize that plans exist in a hierarchy that covers all levels of the organization and, to some extent, are related to what is going on in other health services organizations in the area. The key thought is that all of these plans are interrelated. It is imperative that plans along this hierarchy be compatible and mutually supportive.

Proper attention to these four points should result in plans that are objective, structured, and yet flexible. It is very likely that the extent to which plans are developed with these elements in mind is a measure of their probable success. Managers and workers of all kinds share a common inclination to react negatively to pressures. These negative reactions invariably create blocks to effectiveness. Many pressures can be avoided by good planning that provides an orderliness that is the antithesis of pressure.

With these thoughts as background, we can turn our attention to the two things that the manager must accomplish in planning: setting objectives and developing methods for achieving them.

SETTING OBJECTIVES

By definition, the initial step in planning is the determination of objectives. Unless one knows *what* is to be accomplished it makes no sense to worry about *how* to accomplish it. Objectives can be, and are, set for the entire health services organization, but they are also established for units within the organization. In a very real sense the key to the entire management process (as well as the planning function) is objectives. The management process must begin with the specification of objectives and end with an evaluation of how well they were accomplished.

In setting objectives at the level of the health services organization, the institution must have a basic philosophy. To establish it, certain questions must be asked and answered. Examples include: What are the health needs of the citizens in our society? Who should receive health services, to what extent, and from whom? Building on this philosophical outlook, health services organization managers can then determine their own particular objectives by asking and answering such questions as: Which of the general health needs should this organization meet? What group or groups should it serve? What health care services and programs will best meet the needs selected? What special or combined programs are most appropriate? What human abilities, knowledge, and skills are required to carry out the selected programs and activities? What quantities and types of resources are necessary to carry out the programs and activities? And on and on.

When these questions are satisfactorily answered, the managers can set objectives to serve as guides to thought and action within the organization. Knowing the objectives of the entire health services organization permits the managers of the various departments and units within it to establish compatible and supportive objectives. It is important to remember that no manager can effectively plan in a vacuum. The objectives and methods set for each unit must be related to those of other units and to those of the entire organization. This can be visualized in Figure 3–2. The

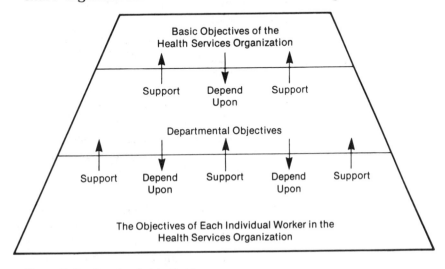

Figure 3–2. Levels of objectives.

reader can see that each set of objectives is related to those above them in the sense that they must be supportive and to those below them in the sense that objectives at lower levels depend on higher level objectives to give them an appropriate sense of direction. It is also clear in Figure 3–2 that objectives down at the level of the individual eventually affect those at the highest level of the organization.

By examining the studies that have been made on setting objectives, a number of conclusions can be drawn that are relevant to the manager in the health services organization:

1. *Individual and departmental objectives must blend with the objectives of the organization.* Theoretically, everyone in the organization should have specific work objectives that are part of the larger plan of the department or unit and ultimately the organization as a whole.

2. *Objectives should be progressive if possible.* It is desirable that there be continuity from period to period in setting and achieving objectives.

3. *Objectives should be jointly determined.* This means that a manager must work with his or her subordinates in setting their objectives; he or she must also work with the next manager up the line in determining objectives for the organizational unit. Participation in setting objectives will mean that those who work to achieve them will have a better understanding of their importance and relevance and will therefore be much more likely to exert maximum effort toward their achievement.

4. *Objectives should be measurable whenever possible.* Health professionals are aware of the difficulties in measuring certain aspects of their work, particularly evaluation of the quality of patient care. Nevertheless, many aspects of the work done in health services organizations are measurable in such terms as person-hours, dollars, satisfaction, and ratios of various types. Such measures permit many objectives to be stated in specific, quantifiable terms that allow a realistic evaluation of progress toward the objective.

5. *Provision must be made for formal accountability.* Objectives imply accountability. When objectives are stated in measurable terms, progress toward their achievement can be directly evaluated. The main reason for making objectives specific is to pinpoint accountability. Every organizational participant who has specific objectives and who is given the resources to accomplish them should be held accountable for the results.

6. *Methods are not as important as objectives.* Such a statement must be qualified somewhat when applied in a health care context. There are methods in the radiology department, for example, that define the way in which a certain procedure will be performed. The method may have been found to be the best way to perform the procedure. Allowing deviation from such methods is not what is intended here. The reader should realize that methods are only means to an end. Those responsible for getting a job done should be allowed to alter the means if it will get the job done in a better way. This kind of attitude stimulates everyone's creativity and makes work much more satisfying.

7. *Flexibility must be built into objectives.* Circumstances change and, on occasion, the objectives must change with them. For example, nursing service may have an objective of holding payroll expenditures below a certain level. However, if patient load goes above that which was projected when the objective was set, then the objective will have to be altered to reflect the new circumstances.

Even though the establishment of objectives is the critical first step in the planning function, some managers do not effectively establish meaningful objectives for their areas of responsibility. Stoner has suggested five main reasons for this:[5]

1. *Unwillingness to give up already established alternative objectives.* The decision to establish specific objectives and commit resources to their achievement requires that other alternatives be foregone. Each of us will at times find it difficult to accept the fact that we cannot achieve *all* of the objectives that are important to us. We may be reluctant to make firm commitments to specific objectives in order to avoid the painful task of giving up other desirable objectives.

2. *Fear of failure.* Whenever someone sets a definite, clearcut objective, that person takes the risk that he or she will fail to achieve it. Managers, no less than other people, see failure as a threat to their self-esteem, to the respect that others have for them, and even to their job security. Thus, their fear of failure keeps some managers from taking necessary risks and establishing specific objectives.

3. *Lack of organizational knowledge.* In order to set effective objectives, a manager needs a good working knowledge of

---

[5]James A.F. Stoner, *Management* (Englewood Cliffs, NJ: Prentice-Hall, Inc. 1978), pp. 142-143.

three areas of the organization: (1) the organization as a whole, (2) other subunits of the organization, and (3) his or her own subunit.

No manager can establish meaningful objectives for a subunit without understanding the broad objectives and strategies of the organization. The objectives of the subunit must contribute to the broader objectives of the total organization. A manager who is new in the organization or who does not keep informed about its latest plans will be understandably hesitant to set new objectives because they might conflict with those established by higher-level management.

Similarly, the manager must be aware of the objectives of other subunit managers to avoid establishing objectives that conflict with or duplicate theirs. A manager with an undeveloped or faulty information system may therefore try to avoid objective setting altogether, and, instead, fall back on already established subunit objectives.

4. *Lack of knowledge of the environment.* In addition to understanding the organization's internal environment, the manager needs to understand the external environment—the competition, clients, suppliers, government agencies, and the general public. The opportunities that an organization needs to fulfill its major objectives, as well as the pitfalls it must avoid in order to survive, are in the external environment. Without knowledge of the external environment, managers are apt to become confused about which direction to take and are reluctant to set definite objectives.

5. *Lack of confidence.* To commit themselves to objectives, managers must feel that they and the subunit or organization have the ability to achieve those objectives. Obviously, if the manager lacks self-confidence or confidence in the organization, he or she will hesitate to establish difficult objectives.

These obstacles to the effective formulation of objectives can be overcome. For example,

A manager who is not adequately informed about the organization or external environment can correct this situation by developing a viable information system. Acquiring this knowledge will in turn help, at least in part, to overcome the fear of failure and the lack of self-confidence.

Another way commitment to a specific objective can be increased is by carefully comparing the value of a chosen objective with that of each rejected alternative. Such comparisons are reassuring because they help to convince the person that the chosen objective is superior.

Furthermore, once an objective is established, it can be continually reevaluated in the light of new information from the organization and the external environment and of feedback from other members of the organization. Such reassessments of the objective often not only reinforce the manager's commitment to it but also enable him or her to replace it with a more suitable objective if it should turn out to be unrealistic or lose its viability.[6]

DEVELOPING METHODS

We have defined planning as deciding in advance what objectives should be set and what methods should be developed to achieve them. Objectives are the *ends* toward which the manager must get people to work, and the methods are the *means* of achieving those ends. The manager's planning efforts, once objectives are established, must be turned to the development of methods to accomplish them. In many ways, the work of the manager is a constant search for effective methods to use in achieving objectives. The fact is that it is the methods that largely account for both quality of work and the efficiency with which it is done (recall that we examined the importance of both in Chapter 2).

The dilemma facing managers who must develop methods for achieving objectives is the existence of what can be a very wide range of alternative methods. The manager's task thus becomes establishing a list of possible methods and then choosing from among them. As the experienced manager knows, and as the student will quickly learn, only rarely is there an obvious "best" method. Therefore, decisions have to be made—most often, tough decisions. Decision making is such an important part of developing methods (and since it is also necessary in the performance of all the management functions) that we will devote all of Chapter 4 to this topic. Suffice it to say here that as the manager chooses from among the various methods available to accomplish a particular objective, he or she must consider the cost of a particular method and weigh this against the probable benefits that will result from it. These costs and benefits are not simply the dollars and cents involved but the social and psychological costs as well. Upon considering the costs and benefits of alternative methods, relative to each other, the manager can choose from among alternative methods in an informed manner.

---

[6]*Ibid.*, pp. 143-144.

"MANAGEMENT BY OBJECTIVES"

Peter Drucker, a noted authority on management, coined the phrase "management by objectives" (MBO) to illustrate the central importance of objectives to the effective management of any undertaking.[7] The "management by objectives" idea is simply that every person in an organization should have specific, attainable, measurable objectives that mesh with those of the organization and that each person's performance should be assessed against achievement of these objectives. It is important to note the word mesh. It does not mean that all objectives have to be the same. They must, however, be compatible with each other.

MBO is a process in which superior and subordinate pairs periodically establish objectives for the subordinate; these objectives usually cover a specific time period and there is periodic review to see how well the subordinate has achieved the objectives. The MBO process can be viewed schematically in Figure 3–3.

MBO is not a panacea for managers but it does provide a number of benefits. A survey of managers found the following benefits to be associated with its use.[8]

1. It lets individuals know what is expected of them.
2. It aids in planning by making managers establish objectives and target dates.
3. It improves communication between managers and subordinates.
4. It makes individuals more aware of the organization's objectives.
5. It makes the evaluation process more equitable by focusing on specific accomplishments. It also lets subordinates know how well they are doing in relation to the organization's objectives.

This last benefit, making evaluation more equitable, suggests that individuals' performance can be evaluated by their impact on the achievement of predetermined objectives.

---

[7]Peter F. Drucker, *The Practice of Management* (New York: Harper & Brothers, 1954).

[8]Henry L. Tosi and Stephen J. Carroll, "Managerial Reaction to Management by Objectives," *Academy of Management Journal*, December 1968, pp. 415-426.

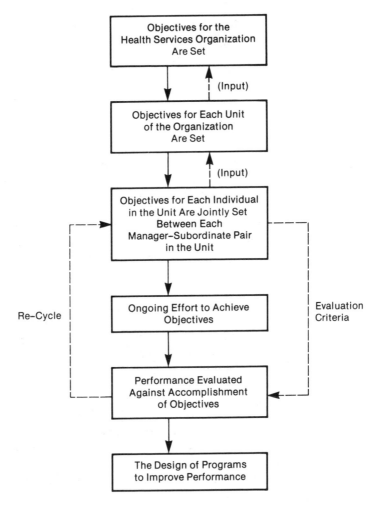

Figure 3–3. The MBO process.

THE IMPACT OF SUCCESSFUL PLANNING

When managers are successful at the planning function, their efforts are of considerable benefit to their organizations. For example, Peters and Tseng have noted, in regard to planning in hospitals, that it forces managers:

> To scrutinize what they do and why they do it. It has broadened the horizons of hospital authorities by encouraging them to look beyond their institutional walls. Planning generates new data on internal

operations and environmental trends and involves more people in long-range thinking. It also imposes a rationality, too often lacking, on institutional decision-making. And, planning provides hospitals with long-term goals and short-range objectives against which progress may be charted and measured.[9]

SUMMARY

Planning is the determination of objectives and the methods for achieving them. It is important to think of planning in one unit of a health services organization as part of a larger whole. For example, the plans of the health services organization to expand must be taken into account in the nursing services' human resources planning. No departmental plan should be made that does not contribute to the objectives set out in the plans of the health services organization. It is the responsibility of top level management in the organization to ensure that all other managers understand the objectives of the organization. It is the joint duty of all managers to determine whether their plans are compatible with all other plans in the organization. If this is done initially, a great deal of trouble can be avoided.

If planning is to be successful, it is essential that plans be properly and effectively communicated to all who are affected by them. All too frequently there is a gap between the knowledge of top administration and lower levels of management with respect to plans. The very essence of planning is informed anticipation of the future. Planning must take place against a background of information and assumptions regarding future conditions that have a bearing on the health services organization.

[9]Joseph P. Peters and Simone Tseng, "Managing Strategic Change," *Hospitals* June 1, 1983, p. 65.

Decision-Making Tools
for the Practice
of Management

FOUR

APRIL 29th
3:00 P.M.

The Operating Room Supervisor and the Chairman of the Department of Surgery sat together, as was their custom, for a few minutes after the last procedure for the day was completed and drank a cup of coffee. They usually discussed the operating schedule for the next day during this time, but today they were on a different subject.

"You know," the Chairman mused, "I've got to find a way to convince our penny-pinching Board of Trustees to expand the intensive care unit."

The Supervisor responded, "I don't see what their problem is. We could fill up twice as many ICU beds as we have—and they charge more than $600 a day for them. I would think they could make a lot of money for the hospital by expanding the ICU."

"They could," the Chairman replied, "but they are on this cost-benefit kick, and the numbers showed that they could get a bigger bang-for-the-buck by spending money on expanding the outpatient clinic."

"Since when have the decisions on life and death been made on the basis of money?" the Supervisor questioned.

"I guess since it became so scarce."

"Well, it's no way to run a hospital. The word around the Nursing Service is that if this fellow, Luther Fillerey, had been in ICU where he belonged, he wouldn't have died."

"We'll never know for sure about that," the Chairman cautioned, "but you probably have a point."

"I know I have a point! When we start making decisions on the basis of bang-for-the-buck around here, quality flies out the window."

"Maybe I can use that argument to get the ICU expanded. The Board has to listen when I tell them that Fillerey died because the ICU was too full to take him. That lawsuit is going to cost them plenty."

At 3:10 p.m. the Chairman reached for the operating schedule for the next day and said, "Well let's see what's coming up for tomorrow."

INTRODUCTION

Decision making is a central aspect of planning. Yet it is not limited to the planning function. It permeates all the management functions—planning, organizing, directing, coordinating, and controlling. It is difficult to think of anything a manager might do that does not have a relationship to a decision made somewhere. Some authorities believe that decision making is a synonym for management. Charns and Schaefer have concluded that "the work of management is to increase the degree to which decisions made by members are organizationally rational."[1]

There have been a number of attempts to describe how practicing managers make decisions. Two views of this have dominated the literature: the *economic man* model and the *administrative man* model. The classic economic man model makes the underlying assumptions that the decision maker will know the alternatives available in a given situation, the consequences that they will bring, and that he or she will always behave rationally. Under the economic man model, the decision maker will always make a choice so as to maximize some desired value.

Herbert Simon has described a more realistic model of the decision maker, calling him the *administrative man*. Administrative man's decision-making behavior may be summarized as follows:

1. In choosing between alternatives, he attempts to satisfice or look for the one which is satisfactory, or "good enough."
2. He recognizes that the world he perceives is a drastically simplified model of the real world. He is content with this simplification because he believes the real world is mostly empty anyway.
3. Because he satisfices, rather than maximizes, he can make his choices without first determining all possible behavior alternatives and without ascertaining that these are in fact all the alternatives.

---

[1] Martin P. Charns and Marguerite J. Schaefer, *Health Care Organizations: A Model for Management* (Englewood Cliffs, NJ: Prentice-Hall, Inc., 1983), p. 234.

4. Because he treats the world as rather empty, he is able to make decisions with relatively simple rules of thumb or tricks of the trade, or from force of habit. These techniques do not make impossible demands upon his capacity for thought.[2]

Simon developed the administrative man model as a more valid model of reality than the economic man model. He argued that the decision maker was never completely informed and was seldom able to maximize anything. Because of these physical limitations of the decision maker, Simon introduced his principle of bounded rationality:

> The capacity of the human mind in formulating and solving complex problems is very small compared to the size of the problem; it is very difficult to achieve objectively rational behavior in the real world ... or even a reasonable approximation to such objective rationality.[3]

Because maximizing is viewed as too difficult for administrative man, Simon suggested that "satisficing" was a more realistic and typical procedure. The satisficer considers possible alternatives until he finds one that meets his minimum standard of satisfaction. Instead of searching a haystack to find the sharpest needle in it, he is content when he finds a needle sharp enough to sew with.

Satisficing is not as complimentary to the decision maker as maximizing, but it is much closer to reality.

DECISION-MAKING DEFINED

Decision making is almost universally defined as *making a choice between two or more alternatives*. This definition has the advantages of being brief and of focusing attention on the essential element of decision making—making a choice. However, to really grasp the nature of decision making, one must understand that making a choice is only one of several sequential steps that must occur as part of an intellectual process. These steps include:

1. Becoming aware that a decision must be made.

2. Defining the problem.

3. Analyzing available information.

---

[2]Herbert A. Simon, *Administrative Behavior* (New York: The Macmillan Publishing Company, Inc., 1947), pp. xxv-xxvi.
[3]*Ibid.*

4. Developing relevant alternative solutions.

5. Choosing the alternative.

6. Converting the chosen alternative into action—execution of the decision. (This step is not technically a part of the decision-making process, but attention must be given to it if management decisions are to be effective.)

This chapter will examine each of these steps in detail and then describe several decision-making tools that can be of help to the health professional who must make management decisions.

Awareness

The most difficult step in decision making, in many cases, is being aware that a decision needs to be made. An effective manager must be sensitive to situations in his area of responsibility that do not meet standards and expectations. This sensitivity can be termed *perceptual skill*, and it enables the manager to collect and interpret cues from his surroundings. When no triggering cues are picked up by the manager, no decision will be made. The manager with limited perceptual skills goes along oblivious to potential problems until they blossom into full-blown crises. This sort of manager lives his or her life reacting instead of acting. Perceptual skills cannot really be taught by textbook and lecture. They are developed through experience and are thus one of the main reasons that managers usually become more effective with experience.

Definition

The effective manager must be able to distinguish between cause and symptom. As in medicine, failure to make this distinction will inevitably lead to a relapse. Defining the real problem is not always an easy task because what appears to be the problem might only be a symptom. For example, a head nurse might believe she is confronted with a problem of conflicting personalities when two staff nurses are continually bickering and cannot get along with each other. Upon checking into this, the head nurse might find that the real problem is that she has never clearly outlined the functions and duties of each staff nurse, specifying where their duties begin and end. Therefore, what appeared to be a problem of personality conflict was actually one of organization.

Defining a problem is usually a time-consuming task, but it is time well spent. There is no need for a manager to go any further in the decision-making process until the problem has been clearly defined, because nothing is as frustrating as the right solution to the wrong problem. A simple, but effective, way of getting behind the symptom and to the underlying problem is to ask *why*? Thus, the crucial step in decision making is an awareness of the real problem that requires a decision.

Analysis

After the problem—and not just the symptoms—has been defined and there is reasonable assurance that its satisfactory solution will provide a means to a desired end, the manager can take the next step in decision making—analyzing available information. This means assembling the facts that are *relevant* to the decision that must be made. Judgment must be used in deciding what information is to be used as well as what information is available. Great care must be exercised to be as fair and objective as possible in gathering and examining the facts that are used in making a decision.

The most difficult "facts" to deal with are the intangible factors that may be involved and that can play a significant role. These intangible factors are such things as reputation, morale, discipline, and personal biases. It is difficult to be as specific about these facts as about those that are subject to physical measurement of some form. Nevertheless, they must be considered in the decision-making process.

In many situations, it is necessary to ferret out the relevant facts. However, the manager should also realize that many decisions can be based on information already at hand. First, there are those problems that clearly fall within the scope of existing procedures. One of the major functions of a procedure is to provide a predetermined course of action, or, in other words, a solution to problems that keep demanding a decision over and over again. Secondly, there are many problems that fall within the decision maker's range of experience and, therefore, do not require the acquisition of additional information. The manager may possess, as the result of prior experience and training, the factual information and conceptualizations necessary to resolve the question and make a decision. The past experience of a potential new manager is an important criterion. The ability to sythesize these past experiences into a cohesive network of information is useful in solving current problems.

The quality of decisions is directly proportional to the number of *relevant* facts that are gathered and analyzed in reaching a decision. Judgment is required in determining when additional facts are needed or whether it is advisable to make a decision even though all necessary facts have not been acquired or analyzed.

Development of Alternate Solutions

After having defined the problem and analyzed the available information, the decision maker's next step is to search for and develop alternate courses of action. One simple rule should guide the decision maker in this step: the greater the number of alternatives considered, the greater the chance of selecting a satisfactory one.

The decision maker should not always think in terms of "one best solution." More realistically, problems have several solutions that have both positive and negative characteristics. The task is to develop as many satisfactory solutions as possible and from these choose the one that seems "best."

It is during this step in the decision-making process that creative and innovative solutions to problems come into being. Logic and experience play major roles in idea generation, but imagination can also make a significant contribution. The use of imagination, or creative thinking, is of great assistance in all functions of management, but it is particularly valuable in the development of relevant alternatives from which the decision maker can exercise choice.

A key point to remember is that creativity is latent within all of us. Ordinary people under the proper circumstances may create new solutions to problems. These proper circumstances include being able to work in an atmosphere of freedom, trust, and security.

The creative process itself can be viewed as a series of steps including:

1. Personal need.
2. Preparation.
3. Incubation and illumination.
4. Verification.

The fact that a *personal need* to think creatively must exist emphasizes the individual aspect of the creative thinking process. It also implies that there must be a motivating force to initiate the creative thought process. This motivation may be a need of self-expression or the result of an externally imposed problem situation.

Contrary to what many people believe, very few creative ideas come as a "bolt from the blue." Rather, they usually grow out of an intensive period of *preparation* during which the decision maker becomes saturated with information and makes a concerted effort to perceive new and meaningful relationships. To a large extent, the originality of ideas depends upon the number of avenues explored and the extent to which all possible interrelationships and solutions are considered. This preparatory step represents the "work" of the creative process.

It is possible for an original solution to a problem to be found quickly as the result of a brief period of analysis. Sometimes this is necessary. However, there is a real need for the concept of *incubation*—a period of mulling the problem over, sometimes consciously and sometimes completely unaware of the thinking process. The value of an incubation period lies in the fact that a more fully developed or more fully illuminated idea may result.

It is helpful to set a deadline for the incubation period so that problems do not go unsolved for unduly long periods of time while the manager hopes for an illumination. However, it is true that some period of incubation is usually necessary for original solutions to be developed.

The final step in the creative thinking process is *verification*. When a solution is first envisioned, especially through the insight of illumination, it is usually not in a polished and final form. The verification step is a period of refining an idea, changing it, and improving it. In effect, it represents the difference between an idea and a creative thought that can be implemented.

The foregoing discussion of the creative process emphasizes the individual's role in creativity, especially in regard to illumination. However, it should be pointed out that often the creative process is stimulated by group effort. This is the underlying basis for brain-storming as an effective method of solving problems.

Brainstorming can be a simple process, but certain guidelines may be useful:[4]

1. Hold the session to about 40-60 minutes in length.

2. Do not reveal the problem before the session begins.

3. State the problem clearly and not too broadly.

4. Use a conference table that allows the participants to communicate easily with each other.

5. If the matter discussed is a physical product, bring along a sample which can be used as a point of reference.

---

[4]Richard M. Hodgetts and Dorothy M. Cascio, *Modern Health Care Administration* (New York: Academic Press, 1983), p. 67.

Relying upon the creative process, experience, perhaps brain-storming with others, and logic, the decision maker should try to visualize as many different solutions to a particular problem as possible; this increases the chance of selecting a good alternative.

Choosing the Alternative

After the decision-making manager has developed and evaluated the alternatives, he must select that alternative he thinks is best. Although he can seek the assistance of specialized personnel and various decision-making aids such as those described later in this chapter, the choice is most often his alone. If the other steps in the decision-making process have been properly carried out, the manager will usually have to choose from several alternatives. One choice that is always available is to do nothing. This should be the most carefully considered choice of all. The decision maker should visualize the consequences that would result from taking no action. Only if the decision to take no action will result in the most desirable consequences should it be selected as the best course of action. The manager should never view the no-action decision lightly or feel that things will remain unchanged as a result of it. After all, something necessitated the need for the decision-making process to take place.

Making the correct choice is not easy. Management decisions tend to be gray rather than black or white. They are usually made in the context of a constantly changing environment; this means that the correct choice now may not remain the most desirable choice.

There are several bases upon which the choice can be made. Among them are: experience, intuition, advice from others, experimentation, and scientific decision making. The whole purpose of the choice is to select the alternative that has the greatest number of desired, and least number of undesired, consequences. Making the best choice is not easy, even when all the bases suggested above are considered. Aside from the element of change, which will affect any decision that is made, there is a problem of incomplete and unavailable information. Also, personal prejudice and bias on the part of the manager can cripple his effectiveness as a decision maker by forcing him to choose an alternative that fits some preconceived notion.

The largest stumbling block to making a choice among alternatives is indecisiveness. Often this stems from feelings of personal inadequacy and insecurity, and these feelings are reinforced by pressure from superiors in the organization. The opposite situation can exist and may be just as detrimental to the effectiveness of the decision maker. This is impulsiveness or a tendency to jump headlong into a situation without considering all factors. It is not uncommon for a young, inexperienced manager to be impulsive in his first decisions; however, if enough of them turn out to be wrong, he may then become indecisive. In either case he is of little value to the health services organization.

There is no simple way to ensure that decisions will be sound ones. However, if the manager will stop and ask himself three questions regarding the decision he is about to make, he can improve its quality considerably.

First, he should ask himself whether or not the decision contributes to the attainment of stated objectives. This implies that the decision is but a means to an end—an end that has been clearly thought out and stated in the form of an objective. If a potential solution does not support stated objectives, it should not be adopted.

Secondly, the decision maker should ask himself whether or not the decision represents a high degree of economic effectiveness. In other words, does the proposed solution make maximum use of available resources? There may be times, of course, when economics should not be used as a criterion for decision making, especially in a health services organization where quality considerations are so important. Usually, however, the economic consideration is a useful guideline.

Finally, the decision maker should ask himself whether or not a potential solution is feasible or capable of execution. In answering this question, the decision maker must think in the very practical terms of how a particular decision will be implemented in view of the resources available.

These considerations do not guarantee that the best decision—or even a good decision—will be made. They do increase the chances for a good decision and are thus worth the effort.

Execution

The process of converting the selected decision into action is not technically a step in the decision-making process. However, the manager will be evaluated more on the outcome of his decisions than on the decisions themselves. The manager must live with his decisions. He must also view each decision as part of a continuum. Once a decision is made and implemented, it will lead to other situations that require decisions. The good manager will use his experience with executing decisions as a means of self-evaluation and self-improvement. He will learn from his mistakes and his successes. The important point is that a decision, from the manager's point a view, is not really complete until it has been executed and then finally appraised.

DECISION-MAKING TOOLS

One of the most striking changes in management practice has been a steady increase in the development and use of quantitative decision-making tools. We cannot hope to cover all of them in detail. Yet it is important to be familiar with some of them; they can make decision making easier and more effective.[5]

Decision Grid

The most basic (and in many ways one of the most useful) decision-making tool is the *decision grid*. This is nothing more than a display of the possible alternatives in a decision along with the various elements that will affect it. Figure 4–1 illustrates a decision grid where the decision involves an executive heart care program. The alternatives are listed down the left-hand margin with the elements affecting the decision making up the rest of the grid. The grid's main advantage is that all pertinent information can be displayed. This becomes especially important in complex decisions and when a committee or other group is working with the decision.

Payoff Tables

An advance over the decision grid can be made if probabilities can be determined for the various possible outcomes of each alternative in a decision. For example, suppose the operating room supervisor is concerned about how many disposable syringes of a certain type should be ordered and stocked each week. Assume that she has determined that there is an 80% probability that she will need 800 syringes and a 20% probability that she will need

---

[5]The interested reader can find a good treatment of quantitative decision making in D. Michael Warner and Don C. Holloway, *Decision-making and Control for Health Administration* (Ann Arbor, MI: Health Administration Press, 1978) and in Kenneth E. Warner and Bryan R. Luce, *Cost-Benefit and Cost-Effectiveness Analysis in Health Care: Principles, Practice and Potential* (Ann Arbor, MI: Health Administration Press, 1982).

Alternative	Effect on Mortality	Effect on Disability	Relative Cost	Feasibility	Desirability and Acceptance	Summary	Decision
1. Present system: Treatment of acute cardiac episodes vs. prevention; inadequate early detection by private physicians	120 deaths per year, 60% considered preventable	800 disability days per year, 50% considered preventable	Dollar cost of preventable portion of morbidity and mortality as expressed in actual dollars expended for medical service: $640,000 per year		Unsatisfactory because known medical and social interventions not used, upping cost	All interested parties persuaded to modify present practices	Not recommended
2. Early detection through screening 80% of target, serology, exercise tests, referral of high-risk patient to own physician	10% reduction of preventable deaths	15% reduction of preventable disability	Cost: $75,000 Return: $69,000	Excellent. Technology and personnel available	Poses minor acceptance problems with patients, but none with attending physicians	Cost high compared with return	Not recommended
3. Above screening plus psychological testing plus recommendation of maintenance regimen to own physician	25% reduction of preventable deaths	30% reduction of preventable disability	Cost: $125,000 Return: $300,000	Requires recruitment and training of clinical psychologists to give screening test	Some resistance on part of patient to be overcome	Greatest return compared with cost. Least coercion of patient or disturbance of doctor-patient relationship	First priority
4. Above program plus group education of high-risk patient in personal care program including diet, exercise, stress prevention, plus continuing education of attending physician	30% reduction of preventable deaths	50% reduction of preventable disability	Cost: $150,000 Return: $350,000	Requires development of education aids, such as films and videotapes. Some delay in implementation	May be difficult to obtain full participation because of lack of interest	Embraces patient responsibility, greatest potential return if screening program discontinued since patient will be motivated to continue	Second priority
5. Above program except quarterly examination, supervised group exercise, education of spouse on diet	35% reduction of preventable deaths	65% reduction of preventable disability	Cost: $300,000 Return: $415,000	Places heavy burden on available manpower	Excessive control and coercion of patient. Voluntary participation not likely to remain at level needed to obtain results	Greatest total return but burden on system and patient excessive	Not recommended

This grid can be used to arrive at a decision on any problem once alternatives are defined and elements selected. At option of the user the elements may be weighted. For example, the relative cost element could be assessed a weighting factor of 2.5 times any other element which would support Alternative 3 as being of first priority.

Figure 4–1. Decision grid, executive heart care program—target population 5,000.

SOURCE: Reprinted, with permission, from *The Practice of Planning in Health Care Institutions*, published by the American Hospital Association, 1973, pp. 56–57.

1,000 syringes in a week. (These estimates are most likely based on past usage patterns.) She can also assign costs to each of these two alternatives. In this case, storage space is allocated at $10.00 per 1,000 syringes. In addition, if she orders and stocks too few syringes, an extra cost of $20.00 will result for special ordering and messenger pickup. Figure 4–2 illustrates the two alternatives

		Events and Results	
		800 (.8)	1,000 (.2)
Decision Quantity (Alternatives)	800	1 $ 8.00	2 $28.00
	1,000	3 $10.00	4 $10.00

Figure 4–2. Payoff table.

(1,000 and 800 syringes) and the costs associated with each at the two outcomes.

For the first alternative, if 800 syringes are stocked and the usage during the week is 800, the costs will be $8.00 (see cell 1). If 800 syringes are stocked and 1,000 are needed that week, the costs will be $28.00 ($8.00 for storage and $20.00 for the special order [see cell 2]).

For the second alternative, if 1,000 syringes are stocked and the usage during the week is 800, the costs will be $10.00 (see cell 3). Also, if 1,000 syringes are ordered and stocked and 1,000 are used, the costs will be $10.00.

If the operating room supervisor orders and stocks 800 syringes, then 80% of the time she will be correct and incur only an $8.00 storage cost; 20% of the time she will not have enough and will have to incur the $28.00 storage and reorder cost. Expected costs can be determined for each alternative as follows:

Expected costs if
800 are ordered $8.00 (0.8) + $28.00 (0.2) = $12.00

Expected costs if
1,000 are ordered $10.00 (0.8) + $10.00 (0.2) = $10.00

Thus, to minimize costs, she would order and stock 1,000 syringes although she would need them only 20% of the time. The reader might ask, "Is all this trouble necessary for a $2.00 savings?" Yes! Two dollars every week is $104.00 per year, *and* there are many items to which this decision technique might be applied. The potential benefits go far beyond this single example.

Obviously, the basic difficulty in using this technique is in determining probabilities. When possible, the preferred procedure is to use historical data or experimental samples so that the probabilities have a clear basis in fact. Where this is not possible, judgment by people who are in the best position to estimate may have to suffice.

Decision Trees

The decision grid and the payoff table presented above give the manager techniques for improving decision making. Yet they suffer from a basic problem—in reality, decisions are seldom one-time affairs. They are more often linked to other decisions in the sense that one decision necessitates future decisions. Decision trees are very useful in evaluating decisions that are linked together over time with various possible outcomes. This technique is especially useful when probabilities can be determined for the possible outcomes.

For example, suppose a clinical laboratory director is faced with a 60% probability that the demand for a certain laboratory procedure will increase by 20% next year and a 40% probability that demand for the procedure will decrease by 10%. The decision is whether or not to buy a piece of automated equipment (at a cost of $50,000) or to pay existing employees overtime wages to do the increased work, should that be necessary. Let's assume that it would be cheaper to pay overtime than to hire an additional worker. Because of the vital nature of the lab procedure, simply deciding not to do the increased work is not acceptable. Figure 4–3 illustrates a decision tree based on this decision. Assume that quality is not an issue here because it will be the same whether the procedure is done manually or on the automated equipment. Thus, the decision hinges on the objective of making the wisest expenditure of money.

Assume that revenue from this procedure is currently $100,000 per year. If the 60% probability of a 20% increase holds up, the revenue for the next year (and future years if everything stays the same) will increase to $120,000; if the 40% probability of a decrease in demand of 10% holds, then revenue will decrease to $90,000 in both cases (see column 3 of Figure 4–3).

The cost of the machine (installation and first year's operation included) is $50,000; the cost of overtime wages is figured at $10,000 if the increased work has to be done and at zero dollars if it does not (see column 4). Net cash flow can be determined in all events by subtracting costs from revenues (see column 5). The expected value at the end of the first year can be obtained in all

(1) Alternative Actions	(2) Possible Events	(3) Revenue from Procedures	(4) Costs	(5) Net Cash Flow	(6) 1st Year Expected Value	(7) Costs	(8) Net Cash Flow	(9) 2nd Year Expected Value
Automate — Increased Demand (.6)		$120,000	$50,000	$70,000	$42,000	$2,000	$118,000	$70,800
Decreased Demand (.4)		90,000	50,000	40,000	16,000	1,500	88,500	35,400
					58,000			106,200
Pay Overtime — Increased Demand (.6)		120,000	10,000	110,000	66,000	10,000	110,000	66,000
Decreased Demand (.4)		90,000	-0-	90,000	36,000	-0-	90,000	36,000
					102,000			102,000

Decision Point

Figure 4–3. Decision tree.

events by multiplying net cash flow (column 5) by the probability of the event. Sixty percent chance of increase times $70,000 equals an expected value of $42,000 (see column 6). At the end of the first year the expected value of automation is $58,000 (42,000 + 16,000) and of paying the overtime is $102,000. Clearly, at that point in time the decision should be to forego the machine and pay overtime. But, if the decision is projected out over additional years this may not be the best decision. Even at the end of the second year (see column 9), the expected value is greater for the decision to automate. Of course, the reader must remember that the initial $50,000 outlay must still be overcome. It won't take many years to do this. By extending the computation this can be determined, and when compared to the expected useful life of the machine, it can form the basis of the final decision.

Cost-Benefit Analysis

As we saw in Chapter 1, the availability of health care resources has come to be acutely strained—to the point that great care must be exercised in the use of those resources. A tool offering considerable promise in this area, if used wisely, is cost-benefit analysis. This tool can be especially useful when trying to decide between alternative expenditures of money. A cost benefit-ratio (Z) is defined as the ratio of the value of benefits of an alternative to the value of the alternative's costs:

$$Z = \frac{\text{present value of economic benefits}}{\text{present value of economic costs}}$$

Several alternatives can be evaluated by comparing the ratios of their benefits and costs. Of course, this ratio is only one factor in the decision, but it can be helpful. It is relatively easy to determine the costs of an alternative. However, frequently in health care situations the value of benefits is much more difficult to determine. What is the value of a human life? What is the value of a higher level of health? Is it better to spend money on making old people more comfortable in their declining years or is it better to spend the money on improving infant mortality rates, and on and on.

Of course, there are many decisions where the costs and benefits of various alternatives can be determined rather easily. In those cases, cost-benefit analysis is a useful tool. For example, suppose the head of a radiology unit is interested in choosing between two pieces of equipment that do essentially the same work. Machine A costs $80,000 (installed) and requires two people to operate it at an annual cost of $24,000 plus $12,000 in non-labor operating costs. The total cost for a year is $116,000. Machine A will produce revenues of $165,000 per year because of its rate of operation. Machine B will have a total cost of $128,000 but will permit revenues of $180,000 because of its rate of operation. Which should be purchased? Assume that they both have the same useful life expectancy and salvage value.

$$\text{Machine A: } Z = \frac{\$165,000}{\$116,000} = 1.422$$

$$\text{Machine B: } Z = \frac{\$180,000}{\$128,000} = 1.406$$

Obviously, if all other things are equal, the best decision is to purchase Machine A.

PERT

The *timing* of decisions is important—in some cases it is the most important aspect of the decision. A tool that is especially helpful in the timing of decisions (on large scale projects particularly) is the Program Evaluation and Review Technique (PERT).

PERT represents a major advance in management practice. It was developed by Booz-Allen-Hamilton, management consultants, and the U.S. Navy as a method to plan and control the Polaris Missile program. The basic tool used in the PERT approach is the network, or flow, plan. The network is composed of a series of related events and activities. *Events* are required sequential accomplishment points in the program or project. *Activities* are the time-consuming elements of the program and actually connect the various events.

For example, suppose a hospital is planning to establish an open-heart surgery unit. A number of events and activities will have to take place. Among them are: renovation of an existing operating room, installation of new equipment, hiring and training an open-heart surgery team, and many others. When many events and activities are involved, PERT can be very useful in planning and controlling (making decisions about) them. In a project of this type, the decision maker might begin by renovating the operating room, then purchasing and installing equipment, then hiring and training the team. Obviously, there is a basic weakness in this approach—namely, the events and activities will be strung out for an unnecessarily long time, thus delaying the project. PERT is a tool that can eliminate this problem.

Figure 4—4 illustrates a PERT Network for the development of an open-heart surgery unit. Events are represented by boxes in the network; activities are represented by arrows connecting events. It should be noted that some events may depend on only a single prior event while, in other situations, there may be an interrelationship of several events leading to the accomplishment of an ultimate objective.

Figure 4—4 illustrates the three basic characteristics of a program or project that is amenable to the PERT approach. The first characteristic is that activities must be such that time estimates can be made. In the example, it is possible to estimate how long it will take to accomplish each activity. Second, there must be definite starting and ending points. Without them, there could be no events that are the beginning or ending of an activity. Finally, and this is the key to PERT's usefulness, there must be parallel activities. That is, several activities must be taking place simultaneously for PERT to be of any real value. This fact will become clear as we proceed.

To make the network understandable and usable, the time between the various events (activity time) must be computed. As anyone concerned with large-scale projects knows, it is not always possible to estimate accurately how long it will take to complete the various parts of the project. However, a method does exist whereby a fairly accurate estimated time between events can be determined.

This approach involves estimating three different times for each activity:

1. *Optimistic Time.* This occasionally happens when everything goes right. The estimate is predicated on minimal and routine difficulties in the activity.

2. *Most Likely Time.* It represents the most accurate forecast based on normal developments. If only one estimate were given, this would be it.

3. *Pessimistic Time.* This is estimated on maximum potential difficulties. The assumption here is that whatever can go wrong will go wrong.

The characteristics of these three time estimates are best described by a beta curve as in Figure 4–5.

A formula based on the probability distribution of time involved in performing the activity is then used. The formula is:

$$\text{Activity Time} = \frac{O + 4M + P}{6}$$

Where O is optimistic time,
M is most likely time, and
P is pessimistic time.

Referring to Figure 4–4, we can see that time estimates between the first two events have been made as follows: optimistic = 5 weeks, most likely = 7 weeks, and pessimistic = 9 weeks. The estimated activity time would then be:

$$t_e = \frac{5 + 4(7) + 9}{6} = 7 \text{ weeks}$$

Using the resulting value, we could be reasonably certain that the activity time between events 1 and 2 will be 7 weeks. The process of calculating activity time must be completed for all activities in the network.

The next step in applying the PERT approach is to determine the *Critical Path.* The Critical Path through the network is the path that takes the longest period of time to complete. In Figure 4–4 the Critical Path is shown by the dashed line. Inasmuch as the Critical Path takes the longest time and is the determinant of project completion, other events that do not lie along the Critical Path may

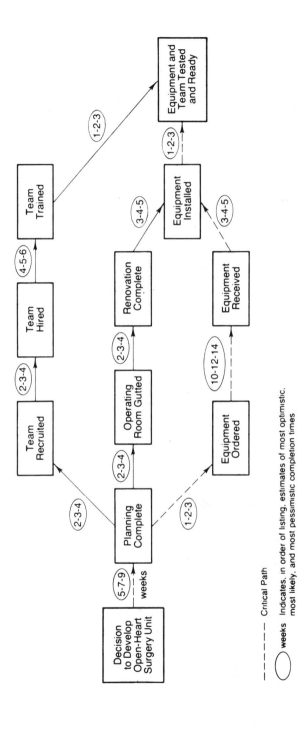

Figure 4–4. PERT network for development of open-heart surgery unit.

- - - - - Critical Path

⬭ **weeks** Indicates, in order of listing, estimates of most optimistic, most likely, and most pessimistic completion times

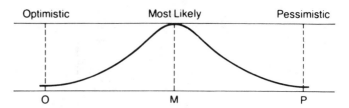

Figure 4–5. Beta curve for optimistic, most likely, and pessimistic time estimates.

be completed before the time they are actually needed. The time differential between scheduled completion of these noncritical events and the time when they are actually required to be completed is called the Slack Time. Where excessive Slack Time exists in the project or program, a reevaluation should take place. It should be determined which resources, and in what amounts, could be transferred to activities along the Critical Path. This may permit the Critical Path, and thus the completion time, to be shortened.

In our example, for instance, it would do no good to speed up recruitment, hiring, or training of the team or the renovation of the operating room *unless* we could reduce time on equipment delivery and installation. The entire process can be speeded up only through those activities since they form the Critical Path.

PERT illustrates the interrelatedness of management functions (especially planning and controlling) and the basic role of decision making. It can be used to great advantage in any building or remodeling project, for the addition of new equipment, for physically moving a department or unit, as well as for many management jobs like budget preparation or policy manual development. The reader who wishes to use the PERT technique will find *Health Program Implementation Through PERT* (By M. Arnold, et al. and published by the Western Regional Office of APHA, 1966) very helpful.

SUMMARY

We have viewed decision making as making a choice between two or more alternatives. In this sense it is critical to effective planning, but it also permeates all other functions of management. Some authorities have even suggested that decision making is a synonym for management.

The decision-making process has been viewed as a series of steps including:

1. Becoming aware that a decision must be made.
2. Defining the problem.
3. Analyzing available information.
4. Developing relevant alternative solutions.
5. Choosing the alternative.
6. Converting the chosen alternative into action.

Several decision-making tools, which can be helpful if properly utilized, were described in this chapter. Most basic is the decision grid, which is a display of the possible alternatives in a decision along with the various elements that will affect it. Payoff tables are an advance over the decision grid in those situations where probabilities can be assigned to various possible outcomes. The decision tree illustrates the necessity, in many cases, of realizing that decisions are not one-time affairs. They are more often linked in the sense that one decision necessitates future decisions. The decision tree is a tool that can be helpful in evaluating decisions linked together over time with various possible outcomes. Cost-benefit analysis is a tool with great potential for the decision maker so long as he or she recognizes the difficulty in determining the true costs and benefits of various alternatives. Finally, PERT is an important tool in the timing of decisions.

Many factors enter into decision making, including: experience, intuition, advice from others, experimentation, and scientific decision making. The effective manager will take advantage of all of these aids to make the vital decisions of what is to be done, by whom, where, and how.

Organizing: The Framework for Management

FIVE

The Hospital Administrator stood up and extended his hand as the Professor from a local university entered his office. They shook hands and exchanged brief pleasantries before they got down to the business at hand.

"The reason I've asked you to come in for this consultation is that I know about your reputation as an expert on organization design, and I've talked with some of my colleagues you've helped. I think some of my problems with managing here at Memorial Hospital result from our organization structure, and I'd like your advice on how we should be set up."

The Professor, whose research had centered on organization design for many years, listened intently. After the Administrator had described the organizational set-up at Memorial and showed him a copy of the organization chart, the Professor asked, "What kinds of problems are you having with this organization design—or, more precisely, what kinds of problems do you think it causes for you?"

"For one thing," the Administrator replied, "all fourteen Department Heads report to me. They include everybody from the Executive Housekeeper to the Director of Nursing. The range of problems they bring to me is something you wouldn't believe."

"There is sometimes a problem with having too many people reporting to one manager," the Professor said as he nodded knowingly.

"It's just impossible for me to keep on top of things when so many people demand my time with so many different kinds of problems. Sometimes I think I've created a monster here—a monster I've lost control over."

"What do you mean?"

"Well, for example, we've got a million dollar lawsuit pending against us for a patient who died here—you may have known him— Luther Fillerey?"

"I knew of him but I didn't know him personally. I hear he was quite a businessman."

"Yes, he was, and I believe that his death is at least partly a result of the fact that I just can't keep on top of everything—we've grown so large that I have to rely on other people to see that things go the way they should—obviously, they don't always!"

"I think I understand your concern, and I can offer some advice on the way an organization such as Memorial Hospital should be structured," the Professor replied.

They set up a series of meetings to discuss this matter. The Professor left at 10:30 a.m., and as he walked through the outer office, he noticed three other people waiting to see the Administrator.

INTRODUCTION

Once the objectives and the methods to achieve the objectives have been established through the planning function, the manager must develop an intentional pattern of relationships among people so that the methods to achieve the objectives can be utilized. The resulting structure is called the *organization,* and the developmental efforts are called the *organizing function* of management. A very important fact about organizations is that they are built in two ways. On the one hand, managers develop the set of relationships among people to a large extent. They decide who will have the responsibility for particular work and who will report to whom and so on. This pattern of relationships, developed by management, is termed the *formal organization.* On the other hand, given the way people in groups behave, there will also be an informal pattern of relationships that emerges because the people, and not necessarily the managers, want them. This arrangement is termed the *informal organization.* Thus, every organization will have two basic parts: a formal structure developed by management and an informal structure that reflects the wishes and preferences of the people who make up the organization. This chapter will concentrate on the formal organization. Chapter 6 will treat the very important topic of the informal organization. Both chapters must be considered together for a complete understanding of the organizing function.

As we noted in Chapter 2, there is no one "best" way to organize that can be generally applied to every situation. The manager must follow a contingency approach and let the variables in a particular situation dictate the choice of a particular organization design. Obviously, in any particular situation, a wide range of variables will have to be considered. Three of the most important have already been touched on: objectives, methods, and people. The objectives and the methods used to achieve them can be quite different from one situation to another. The manager of the admissions department of a hospital has one set of objectives and methods, and these will be different from those of other departments such as the pharmacy or the dietary department. Similarly, the objectives and methods developed for a major medical center will be different from those of a small group practice of physicians, and both will be different from those of a small hospice. The variation in the "people" variable is quite literally limitless. Some people need and want clearly defined work of a routine nature and may require careful and close supervision of their efforts to do their best work; others may prefer a high degree of freedom in choosing how they will work and will resist close supervision. In between these extremes lie an almost infinite variety of preferences in terms of how people would like to work. Thus, we can see that the manner in which a manager carries out the organizing function can be affected by many variables—primarily the objectives that are sought, the methods that are used, and the nature and preferences of the people who will form the organization. The manager, in carrying out the organizing function, must take these variables into account in the design of an effective and efficient organization.

Poor organization lies at the root of many problems that managers face. For instance, a chief medical technologist described a situation in which two technologists were constantly bickering and arguing. The chief had decided that there was a basic personality conflict between the two. To solve the problem, she was in the process of deciding how to terminate one of the technologists. Both were fairly productive workers, but their actions were disruptive and threatened to involve other workers. The chief technologist, in discussing the situation, realized that the arguments might be a symptom and not the problem. She discovered that the real problem was that the relationship between them had not been *organized* properly (by clearly delineating the work responsibility of each technologist). When this was done, most of the problem cleared itself up and she had two workers who did their work and got along reasonably well. This situation repeats itself many times over in the typical health services organization. While personality conflicts do exist, they are often caused by poor organization.

Essentially, the organizing function grows out of the human need for cooperation. When one considers the complexity of the typical health services organization with its varied activities and the diversity of the people who perform those activities, it is clear that the necessity for organization exists in these organizations to a greater degree than in almost any other type of organization in our society.

Even in a single unit of the health services organization, such as the nursing service or the radiology department, there is such a wide range of work performed by people of several skill levels that organization is a vitally important aspect of overall effectiveness and efficiency. These two concepts, *effectiveness* and *efficiency,* although different, must be considered together because they are both important. An organization structure is *effective* if it facilitates the contribution of individuals in the attainment of the objectives that have been set. It is *efficient* if it facilitates the accomplishment of objectives with a minimum of cost. Thus, it is possible to be effective but not efficient or vice versa. The manager must keep both concepts in mind in the organizing function, especially in view of the growing and concurrent demands for high quality services and containment of the costs of those services.

It is easy to see the need for organizing at the level of the institution, where so many people and functions are involved, but it is equally important to organize at each level down to and within the departmental level.

To the manager at the departmental level, organization must therefore be viewed from two perspectives. He must be concerned about the organization as a whole and how he relates to it. He must also be concerned about the internal organization of the department. He should realize, however, that the same principles underlie the organizing function in both cases.

ORGANIZATION THEORY

Much as in medicine, modern management practices have evolved over time from earlier approaches. Present theory and knowledge about the organizing function owes a twofold debt to those early researchers and practitioners who sought the "best" approaches to the organizing function. On the one hand, some of the early developments of what has come to be called the *classical* approach are still in use today, and on the other hand, much of the *modern* approach has emerged as a reaction to, or improvement over, the shortcomings of the classical approach. Thus, to really understand the organizing function, the manager must know about the work of the classical theorists *and* the modern theorists because the two approaches are intertwined. The classical theory, with its shortcomings, serves as a basis for understanding the modern approach to the organizing function.

CLASSICAL ORGANIZATION THEORY

Williams has summarized the importance of classical organization theory very well:

Most organizations are strongly influenced by classical theory. Some of its assumptions are questionable, many of its principles are deficient, its assertions are too sweeping, and its application has often led to undesirable results. It is, nevertheless, a brilliant expression of organization theory and a standard of reference which cannot be ignored or considered insignificant by theorist or practicing manager.[1]

The literature base for the classical approach emerged largely during the first half of the twentieth century with the writing of such people as Fayol, Gulick, Urwick, Mooney, and Reiley.[2]

One of the major developers of classical organization theory was Max Weber (1864–1920), a German sociologist, who is most often associated with the organization concept of bureaucracy. His work is a logical beginning point in the analysis of the organizing function because, in its pure form, Weber thought that bureaucracy represented an ideal or completely rational form of organization.[3]

The Bureaucratic Model

The term *bureaucracy* stimulates a negative image in the minds of many people. It has come to represent the undesirable characteristics of "red tape," duplication, delay, and general frustration found in many large organizations. The term, as used by Weber, meant something entirely different. He used it to describe an ideal organization structure based on the sociological concept of rationalization of collective activities. Weber's concept of bureaucracy was an "ideal" type because he abstracted the concept from observations of actual organizations; however, no real-world organization exactly follows the Weber model. Peter M. Blau has summarized Weber's conception of bureaucracy as follows:

Weber dealt with bureaucracy as what he termed an ideal type. This methodological concept does not represent an average of the attributes of all existing bureaucracies (or other social structures), but a

---

[1]J. Clifton Williams, *Human Behavior in Organizations* (Cincinnati, Ohio: South-Western Publishing Co., 1978), p. 26.

[2]For example see: Henri Fayol, Trans. Constance Storrs, *General and Industrial Management* (London: Sir Isaac Pitman and Sons, Ltd., 1949); Luther Gulick and Lyndall Urwick (eds.), *Papers on the Science of Administration* (New York: Institute of Public Administration, 1937); Lyndall Urwick, *The Elements of Administration* (New York: Harper and Row Publishers, Inc., 1943); James D. Mooney and Alan C. Reiley, *Onward, Industry!* (New York: Harper and Brothers, 1931); James D. Mooney, *The Principles of Organization* (New York: Harper and Brothers, 1947).

[3]Max Weber, *The Theory of Social and Economic Organization*, Trans. A. M. Henderson and Talcott Parsons (New York: Oxford University Press, 1947).

pure type, derived by abstracting the most characteristic bureaucratic aspects of all known organizations.[4]

Bureaucratic Characteristics

To achieve the maximum benefits of an ideal bureaucracy, Weber believed that an organization must be characterized by the following:

1. A clear division of labor exists, so that each task to be performed by employees is systematically established and legitimatized by formal recognition as an official duty.
2. The functions within the organization are officially arranged in a hierarchial manner. That is, a chain of command from the top down is established.
3. The actions of employees are governed by rules and procedures which are formally prescribed and which are utilized in a uniform manner in every situation.
4. The officials of the bureaucracy apply the rules and procedures as impersonally as is humanly possible. The "people" element is given consideration after the entity itself.
5. Employment in the bureaucracy is based upon rigid selection criteria which apply uniformly and impersonally to each candidate applying or being considered for a position. The criteria for selection are based upon objective standards for the job which have been established by the officials of the organization.[5]

Classical Principles of Organization

In much the same way that Weber's bureaucratic model of the organization was an attempt to describe the "ideal" organization, the classical theorists sought a set of universal principles that could be used in guiding the design of any organization. The main classical principles that will be described here include: specialization of labor, departmentalization, span of control, equal authority and responsibility, delegation, and unity of command.

Specialization of Labor

The classical theorists (and even before them, the economist Adam Smith) recognized the benefit of permitting each worker to specialize in the performance of a relatively few methods. The benefit is that each specialized worker can then become proficient and efficient in the performance of his work. Health services organizations, as we noted in Chapter 1, utilize the talents of a tremendous

---

[4]Peter M. Blau, *Bureaucracy in Modern Society* (Chicago: University of Chicago Press, 1950), p. 34.

[5]Max Weber, "The Essentials of Bureaucratic Organization: An Ideal-Type Construction," in R. K. Merton, et al., eds., *A Reader in Bureaucracy* (Glencoe, IL: The Free Press, 1952), pp. 18-27.

array of workers—most of whom have developed particular specialties so that they can function in the complex health services organizations. The positive benefits of specialization (increased proficiency and efficiency) are, however, somewhat offset by certain problems. When work becomes excessively specialized, those who perform it often become bored. Sometimes specialists in one area cannot easily communicate with specialists in another area because they develop their own "languages." Finally, when a person becomes a specialist, he frequently feels that it is important to protect the boundaries of his specialty from encroachment by others.

Departmentalization

A direct outgrowth of having organization participants who are highly specialized is the need to group them together on this basis (usually called the *functional* basis of departmentalization) so that all those performing similar functions are grouped together in a single unit or department. Thus in a hospital, nurses are in the nursing department, pharmacists are in the pharmacy department, and so on. Even within a department, the concept underlying the departmentalization principle can be followed to break the department down into smaller units. For example, a large clinical laboratory (which can be thought of as a functionally specialized department) may have even more functionally specialized and grouped units such as a blood bank, a chemistry section, and a hematology section, to name a few.

The single most important advantage of functional departmentalization is that it incorporates the benefits of specialization. Of course, it carries with it the possible dysfunction sometimes built up by departmental empires that conflict to the point of detracting from the organization's overall performance. Also, the problems of coordination become more complex as departments multiply. We will examine the function of coordination in depth in Chapter 8. The reader should note that this is another example of the interrelatedness of the functions of management: what is done in organizing affects what is done in coordinating.

Span of Control

Span of control may be defined simply as the number of subordinates reporting directly to a superior. The classicists were in general agreement that there should be a limited number of subordinates reporting to a superior. Some of them even went so far as to attach specific numbers to the optimum span. More recent thinking suggests that there is no predetermined number of people that a manager can effectively supervise. It should be noted that the number of relationships existing between a superior and each possible combination of subordinates goes up at a startling rate as the number of subordinates increases. For example, if there are only five subordinates, the number of possible relationships between the superior and some combination of subordinates is thirty-one. If the number of subordinates is doubled to ten, the number of relationships that are possible jumps to 1,023! If follows from this that a manager should be more effective in dealing with a relatively small number of subordinates than with a large number. Several factors enter into the question of span of control. The level in the organization has a great deal to do with determining a suitable span. At the top level five or six subordinates may be all that should exist. At a lower level, where work tends to be more standardized and routinized, fifteen may not be too many. Another factor is the nature of the work being performed. It is easier to supervise ten file clerks than five head nurses. The abilities and availability of managers should also be taken into account. Obviously, the training and personal qualities of some managers permit them to handle more subordinates than others, thus facilitating a broader span. Similarly, the greater the training, capacities, and self-direction of subordinates, the fewer relationships they will need with management and the more subordinates a given manager can handle.

As Massie and Douglas have pointed out, the classical view of span of control refers to concern over the number of people a manager can directly *supervise*. This is not the same thing as the span of management *responsibility*, "which refers to the number of people one superior can assist, teach, and help reach their objectives—that is, the number who *have access* to the superior."[6] It is quite likely that the span of management responsibility can be larger than the span of control.

Equal Authority and Responsibility

In the view of the classicists, the legitimization of authority at a central source ensures that the superior "has the *right* to command someone else and that the subordinate person has the *duty* to obey the command. This is implied in the notion of official legitimacy, legal in nature rather than social and informal."[7]

The classical principle states that there must be an equal relationship between the responsibilities of a manager and the authority that he exercises. Urwick has noted:

---

[6]Joseph L. Massie and John Douglas, *Managing: A Contemporary Introduction*, 2nd ed. (Englewood Cliffs, NJ: Prentice-Hall, Inc., 1977), p. 143.

[7]John M. Pfiffner and Frank P. Sherwood, *Administrative Organization* (Englewood Cliffs, NJ: Prentice-Hall, Inc., 1960), p. 75.

To hold a group or individual accountable for activities of any kind without assigning to him or them the necessary authority to discharge that responsibility is manifestly both unsatisfactory and inequitable. It is of great importance to smooth working that at all levels authority and responsibility should be conterminous and coequal.[8]

The principle of equal authority and responsibility does not provide a formula by which one can equate them. In fact, no sure formula exists. Yet this fact does not negate the basic premise that if one is given a responsibility in the organization, he must also be given the authority to fulfill it. As has been noted however, "in many instances health care managers find that their responsibility is indeed greater than their authority. They are charged with the efficient operation of their unit or department but find their hands are tied when it comes to making decisions for straightening out the situation."[9]

Delegation

Another classical principle of organization is based upon the fact that no one person can accomplish or even be directly responsible for the establishment and achievement of all of the objectives of a complex organization. Thus, there must be delegation or assignment of authority and responsibility to others in the organization. If departments and units made up of functionally specialized workers have been created, then they should be delegated the responsibility for performing those functions; they should be delegated the authority (over use of resources for example) necessary to perform them; and, finally they should be held accountable for performing them. Delegation serves several positive purposes. By delegating those things that can be, the manager frees up her own time for other matters that cannot be delegated. If delegation is made as far as—but no further than—it should be, then those people in the organization who are best qualified will be responsible for accomplishing the work involved. Finally, subordinates are given the opportunity to reach their maximum level of contribution to the organization when they are delegated responsibility and authority consistent with their abilities.

Unity of Command

This classical principle suggests that the organization is a series of relationships between superiors and subordinates in which each subordinate takes orders from one, and only one, superior. This principle is related to the authority-responsibility principle de-

---

[8]Urwick, *Elements of Administration*, p. 46.

[9]Richard M. Hodgetts and Dorothy M. Cascio, *Modern Health Care Administration* (New York: Academic Press, 1983), p. 143.

scribed above in that the grant of authority and the assignment of responsibility should flow to a subordinate through one immediate superior. If taken to their full limit, these concepts result in a chain of command that flows from the top of the organization to the bottom in a scalar fashion.

If one applies these principles in carrying out the organizing function of management, the result will be an organization designed very much like those reflected in the organization charts of the hospital or the nursing home given in Chapter 1. (Go back and review Figure 1–9 and Figure 1–10.) The organization charts depicting the design of the formal organization in both cases are tangible evidence that these principles are usually followed in designing health services organizations. If the principles are applied to the design of a single department in a health services organization, the results are equally predictable. For example, Figure 5–1 is a partial organization chart that would result from applying these principles to the design of a clinical laboratory department.

MODERN ORGANIZATION THEORY

The application of the classical principles of organization described above accounts for the structural design of almost all health services organizations—indeed, of almost all formal organizations in the Western world. This does not mean, however, that the organizing function is simply the application of these principles. The classical principles have been criticized on a number of bases. These criticisms have spawned modifications of and alternatives to the classical approach. Beginning in the 1940's and continuing into the 1950's, a number of writers and researchers began to question seriously the classical principles, primarily on the basis of the underlying assumptions held by the classicists about human beings in the work place. To counter what they saw as an inappropriate view of the human element in the classical approach, these writers and researchers worked to build a better understanding of the role and behavior of people in formal organizations. Since they did not entirely reject the classical approach but sought to resolve what they saw as its main shortcoming, they have been called the *neoclassicists*.

The major criticisms of the classical approach—the ones which the neoclassicists sought to correct—have been summarized by Stoner as follows:

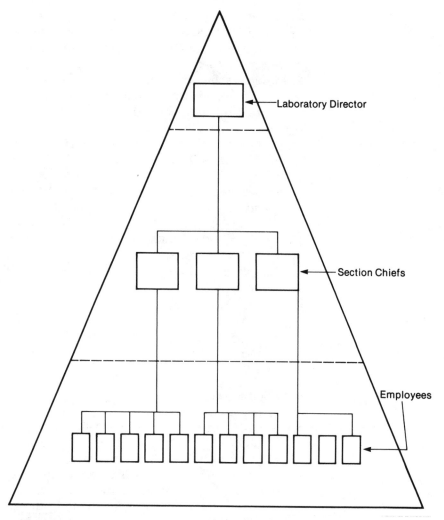

Figure 5–1. Organization chart of a clinical laboratory.

1. It neglects the human aspects of organization members, who are assumed to be motivated only by basic economic incentives. As the educational levels, affluence, and work expectations of organization members have risen over time, this criticism has become more severe.

2. It does not take into account rapidly changing and uncertain environments. Formalized bureaucratic organizations have difficulty changing their rigidly installed procedures.

3. As the organization grows in size, top managers become progressively out of touch with realities at the lower levels of the organization. This problem is compounded when technology changes rapidly. As new workers enter the organization, they are

likely to have technical skills that surpass those of their superiors higher up in the organization. Some of these differences in technical skills may be offset by the advantages that top managers have in terms of experience, wider perspective, and more access to information at higher levels. Even so, rapid technological changes cast doubt on the assumption that upper-level managers automatically have greater ability than their lower-level counterparts.

4. As organizational procedures become more formalized and individuals become more specialized, the danger increases that the means will become confused with the ends. Specialists, for example, in concentrating on their own finely tuned goals, may lose sight of the fact that these goals are not ends in themselves but a means toward reaching the broader goals of the organization.[10]

The most basic distinction between the classical and neoclassical approaches to the organizing function was in the assumptions made about the nature of human beings in the work place. Douglas McGregor (a neoclassist) has summarized these assumptions in developing what he called *Theory X* assumptions (those held by the classicists) and *Theory Y* assumptions (those held by the neoclassicists). These assumptions can be summarized as follows:[11]

Theory X:

1. The average person has an inherent dislike for work and will avoid it if he or she can.

2. Because of this human characteristic of dislike of work, most people must be coerced, controlled, directed, and threatened with punishment to get them to put forth adequate effort toward the achievement of organization objectives.

3. The average person prefers to be directed, wishes to avoid responsibility, has relatively little ambition, and wants security above all.

Theory Y:

1. The expenditure of physical and mental effort in work is as natural as play or rest.

---

[10]James A. F. Stoner, *Management* (Englewood Cliffs, NJ: Prentice-Hall, Inc., 1978), p. 317. Reprinted by permission of Prentice-Hall, Inc., Englewood Cliffs, New Jersey.

[11]Douglas McGregor, *The Human Side of Enterprise* (New York: McGraw-Hill Book Company, 1960), pp. 33-34, 47-48.

2. People will exercise self-direction and self-control in an effort to achieve objectives to which they are committed.

3. Commitment to objectives is a function of the rewards associated with their achievement.

4. The average person learns, under proper conditions, not only to accept but to seek responsibility.

5. The capacity to exercise a relatively high degree of imagination, ingenuity, and creativity in the solution of organizational problems is widely, not narrowly, distributed in the population.

As the reader can see, these assumptions are quite different, and organizations designed by managers who hold the Theory X assumptions are likely to be quite different than those designed by managers who hold the Theory Y assumptions about human behavior in an organizational setting. The Theory Y assumptions give a more realistic view of human behavior in organizations and, to a large extent, represent the major contribution to our understanding of the organizing function made by the neoclassicists. However, a word of caution about Theory Y is in order. McGregor described the "average" human being. The "average" person is a nonexistent, statistical concept. In the real world, some people fit the Theory X model. McGregor's argument is that the Theory Y assumptions describe a far larger proportion of people than was assumed to be the case by the classicists—but not everyone.

In addition to McGregor, other neoclassicists include Abraham Maslow, whose work is so basic to our understanding of human motivation that we will discuss it at length in Chapter 7, where motivation is one of the main topics. The work of the neoclassical theorists has led to *modern organization theory*. The reader is cautioned that the term *modern theory* does not mean that neoclassical theory is now out of date. As Williams has stated, modern and neoclassical organization theories "coexist, interact and in places are indistinguishable."[12] It is useful to view modern organization theory as an emerging, though incomplete, transition from the classical and neoclassical views.

Distinguishing Features of Modern Theory

Two features distinguish modern organization theory. First is its concentration on the organization as an integrated system in which

---

[12]Williams, *Human Behavior in Organizations*, p. 41.

all of the parts are interrelated. Second, after years of searching by the classicists, and many of the neoclassicists, for the "one best way" to structure organizations, the modern view that the structure of an organization should be contingent upon the particular situation in which it finds itself has emerged. As we noted earlier in this chapter, the most important variables that the design must take into account are the objectives of the organization, the methods that will be used to accomplish them, and the people who will utilize the methods. The manager's job, in the modern contingency approach to organization design, is to develop an effective fit between the organization's structure and these variables.

The typical health services organization (go back and review the organization patterns described in Chapter 1) is organized along the classical lines. There is a high level of division of work (as indicated by a high degree of specialization and sub-specialization); there is departmentalization along functional lines; limited span of control along with delegation of authority and responsibility result in the bureaucratic pyramid (although in hospitals there are the two pyramids of administrative and medical staff).

Although the typical health services organization is still organized along the classical lines, some are beginning to make changes in view of the criticisms outlined above. A problem of particular severity has been that of designing an organization structure that brings the health professionals more directly into the management and decision making of the organization. An approach that holds great potential in this area is matrix organization. We will describe the development of matrix organization and see how it might be applied in one health services organization—the hospital.

MATRIX ORGANIZATION

Highly technical industries (aerospace most notably) have begun to utilize *project organization* when management decides to focus a great amount of talent and resources for a given period on a specific project goal. A project "team" of various specialists is put together under the direction of a project manager.

Health services organizations can utilize the project organization concept very easily by superimposing it over their existing functional organization. The result of the superimposition is called *matrix organization*. It provides a horizontal, lateral dimension to the traditional vertical orientation of the functional organization.

Duncan Neuhauser has suggested that hospitals can do this very easily, and in fact, some already have. They do it by establishing patient care teams under the leadership of individual physicians for individual patients.[13] Figure 5–2 illustrates this. The design also shows where the term "matrix" organization comes from.

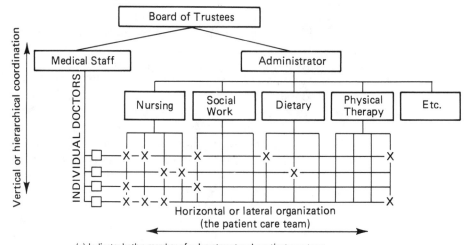

Figure 5–2. The hospital as a matrix organization.

SOURCE: Reprinted, with permission, from the quarterly journal of the American College of Hospital Administrators, *Hospital and Health Services Administration*, Duncan Neuhauser, "The Hospital as a Matrix Organization," Fall, 1972, p. 20.

Johnson and Tingey argue that "although the physician is responsible for the initial formulation of a therapeutic plan (and in that sense, provides direction for the patient care team), bringing the plan to actuality is the function of the nurse. The physician simply is not physically present long enough to coordinate the implementation of patient care programs."[14] This point is an important one. It may well be that for the time being, hospitals that wish to utilize the matrix approach will have to have co-team leaders: a physician and a nurse for each team. This is a good example of the contingency approach to organization design in that it fits the dictates of the particular situation at hand.

---

[13]Duncan Neuhauser, "The Hospital as a Matrix Organization," in Anthony Kovner and Duncan Neuhauser, eds., *Health Services Management: Readings and Commentary*, 2nd ed. (Ann Arbor, MI: Health Administration Press, 1983). Additional information on matrix organization can be found in Joseph E. Ryan, "Better Style for Change: Matrix Management," *Hospitals*, November 16, 1980, pp. 105-108.
[14]G. Vaughn Johnson and Sherman Tingey, "Matrix Organization: Blueprint of Nursing Care Organization for the 80's," *Hospital and Health Services Administration*, Winter, 1976, p. 34.

It should be noted that the matrix organization concept does not do away with the classical organization structure—it simply builds upon it and improves on it. As we pointed out earlier in this chapter, there is no definitive way health services organizations (or any other type of organization) *should* be designed. The technical term, *equifinality*, is very applicable to the organization function. The concept means that final results may be achieved with different initial conditions and in different ways. This view suggests that the organization (or a part of it) can accomplish its objectives with varying inputs and with varying internal activities. It suggests also that the manager can use a varying bundle of inputs into the organization, can transform these in a variety of ways, and still achieve satisfactory output. Extending this view even further suggests that the management process is not necessarily one of seeking a rigid optimal solution to problems but rather one of having available a variety of satisfactory solutions to management problems.

The manager who is trying to organize his area of responsibility can draw upon the classical principles of organization, but he should also be aware that they can, very often, be improved upon.

STAFFING ASPECTS OF THE ORGANIZING FUNCTION

An organization structure can easily be designed on paper. To make the organization come to life it must be staffed. To ensure the organization's effectiveness, it must be staffed with competent people. The process of filling the organization structure with competent people, through selection and development of personnel to fill the roles designed into the structure, is called "staffing." All managers have a responsibility for staffing. When a manager is given responsibility over a particular part of an organization, staffing is one of the central aspects of this responsibility. The organization chart, in conjunction with job descriptions and job specifications, will specify the numbers and types of workers needed to fill the various positions.

The manager will be aided substantially in the staffing process by the services of the personnel department. Usually the personnel department is attached to the health services organization in a staff capacity. This means that its purpose is to counsel, advise, and provide services to the other departments and units in the organization. It is important to remember, however, that the responsibility for staffing rests with the line managers (i.e., those in charge of departments or units) of the organization. Sometimes, in its eagerness to be of service or as the result of a weak manager's abdication of some of his responsibility, the personnel department may assume too large a role in the staffing process. This should be guarded against; if the manager permits the personnel department to make staffing decisions for him, his relationships with his employees will sooner or later be weakened. This is not to say that the personnel department has no importance in the staffing process. Rather, staffing requires a coordinated and balanced effort on the part of the personnel department and the manager. If both realize their responsibilities and carry them out properly, staffing problems can be minimized.

The Staffing Process

Staffing activities result in the appointment of individuals to vacant or newly created organization positions, either by attracting them as candidates for employment from outside the organization or by moving them into the position by promoting or transferring them from within the organization. Successful staffing is a complicated process requiring proper performance of a number of specific steps. Figure 5–3 illustrates these steps and emphasizes their interdependence.

A meaningful treatment of the steps in the staffing process is beyond the scope of this book. It will be useful, however, to describe briefly each step in the staffing process so that the health services manager understands both the importance and the complexity of the staffing process. This description is adapted from James A. F. Stoner:[15]

1. *Human Resource Planning.* Human resource planning is designed to ensure that the personnel needs of the organization will be constantly and appropriately met. Such planning is accomplished through analysis of current and expected skill needs, vacancies, and department expansions and reductions. As a result of this analysis, plans are developed for executing the other steps in the staffing process.

2. *Recruitment.* Recruitment is concerned with developing a pool of job candidates, in line with the human resource plan. The candidates are usually located through newspaper and profes-

---

[15]Stoner, *Management,* pp. 497-498. Reprinted by permission of Prentice-Hall, Inc., Englewood Cliffs, New Jersey.

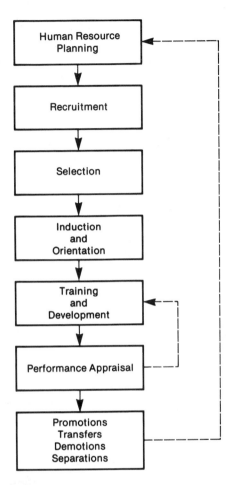

Figure 5–3. The staffing process.

sional journal advertisements, employment agencies, and visits to college and university campuses.

3. *Selection*. The selection process involves evaluating and choosing among job candidates. Application forms, résumés, interviews, and reference checks are commonly used selection devices.

4. *Induction and Orientation*. This step is designed to help the selected individuals fit smoothly into the organization. Newcomers are introduced to their colleagues, acquainted with their responsibilities, and informed about the organization's objectives and methods.

5. *Training and Development*. The process of training and development aims at increasing the ability of individuals and

groups to contribute to organizational effectiveness. *Training* is designed to improve job skills; managers might be instructed in new decision-making techniques or the capabilities of data processing systems. *Development* programs are designed to educate employees beyond the requirements of their present position so that they will be prepared for promotion and able to take a broader view of their roles in the organization.

6. *Performance Appraisal.* This step compares an individual's job performance against standards or objectives developed for the individual's position. If performance is high, the individual is likely to be rewarded (by a promotion, for example, or by more challenging work assignments). If performance is low, some corrective action (such as additional training) might be arranged to bring the performance back in line with desired standards.

7. *Transfer, Promotion, Demotion, Separation.* A *transfer* is a shift of a person from one job, organizational level, or location to another. Two common types of transfers are *promotion*—a shift to a higher position in the hierarchy, usually with added salary, status, authority, and opportunity— and *demotion*—a shift to a lower position in the hierarchy. *Separation,* as the term implies, may involve resignation, layoff, discharge, or retirement. The type and quantity of separations can provide insights into the effectiveness with which the organization is managed. For example, too many resignations might signify a noncompetitive pay scale; too many discharges might indicate poor selection or training procedures; and too many retirements might show poor management of the age mix among organization members.

SUMMARY

The management function of organizing can be defined as relating people and things to each other in such a way that they are all combined and interrelated into a unit capable of being directed toward organizational objectives. In the complex health services organization, this function grows out of the critically important need for cooperation among the various organizational participants.

There is no definitive theory about the way organizations should be designed. The manager is faced with both classical and modern theories. The main point of this chapter is that there are many components of both classical and modern theories of organizational design that are appropriate to the modern health services organization. Several concepts and principles, beginning with Weber's bureaucratic model and including division of work, unity of command, equal authority and responsibility, limited span of control, and delegation, are applicable to some extent in the modern health services organization. However, it is useful to view the application of these principles from a modern perspective. We have done this by emphasizing the concept of matrix organization that does not ignore classical structure but that builds upon it and improves on it.

An organization, no matter how carefully designed, cannot exist on paper. It must be brought to life by filling the various positions with competent men and women. The staffing process is a very important part of the total management function of organizing.

The Informal Aspects
of Organization

SIX

The Medical Records Administrator at Memorial Hospital picked up the telephone receiver and dialed the secretary on the unit where Luther Fillerey had recently died. When the secretary answered, she heard, "Look, I know I'm supposed to go through the Department Heads with a request like this but I just don't have the time to wait for them. I've got to get the medical record for Luther J. Fillerey, patient number 3222–004, completed for the Hospital Administrator—this lawsuit business, you know. Some of the nurses' notes are not signed, and there are some lab and radiology reports that haven't been placed in the record yet. Can you look after this for me? It's important, and I just don't have the time to go through all the channels."

The secretary replied, "Sure, I'll take care of it. Bring the record with you when we meet for lunch, and I'll get it taken care of this afternoon."

"Great! I'll see you in the cafeteria at noon."

It was 11:16 a.m. as the Medical Records Administrator replaced the phone and thought to herself, "It's so easy to get things done when you are on friendly terms with people. That would have taken a week if I had gone through channels. Especially since those people in the lab can be so uncooperative sometimes. Well, on to other things!"

INTRODUCTION

Existing within the formal organization's pattern of authority-responsibility relationships is another equally important structure—the informal organization. As seen in the previous chapter, the formal organization is a planned structure. It represents the deliberate attempt to establish patterned relationships among participants in the organization. A great deal of management time and effort goes into the establishment and maintenance of the formal organization. These efforts include the development of an organization structure as depicted by the organization chart, job descriptions, formal rules, operating policies, work procedures, control procedures, compensation arrangements, and many other devices used to guide employee behavior. However, as people who have particpated in an organization know, there are many interactions between members of an organization that are not prescribed by the formal structure. *These relationships and interactions that occur spontaneously out of the activities and interactions of members of the organization, but that are not set forth in the formal structure, make up the informal organization.*

One of the things that distinguishes the classical organization theorists from the modern theorists (especially the behaviorists) is that the classical thinkers concentrated on the formal organization and the behaviorists have concentrated primarily on informal relationships. This has led to an artificial division of the two (something that is specifically *not* intended by having separate chapters on the two in this book). The formal and informal organizations coexist and are inseparable. They are totally intermeshed. As pointed out by Blau and Scott:

> It is impossible to understand the nature of a formal organization without investigating the networks of informal relations and the unofficial norms as well as the formal hierarchy of authority and the official body of rules, since the formally instituted and the informally emerging patterns are inextricably intertwined. The distinction be-

tween the formal and the informal aspects of organization life is only an analytical one and should not be reified; there is only one actual organization.[1]

NATURE OF INFORMAL ORGANIZATION

Real awareness and interest in the informal organization stemmed from the famous Hawthorne studies of the 1930s.[2] These studies showed that informal organization is an integral part of the total work situation. Since the informal organization arises from the *social interaction* of participants in an organization, it has come to be synonymous with small groups and their patterns of behavior. Most of what managers know about the informal organization has come from the work of sociologists and social psychologists. Many of their contributions will be described in this chapter.

The basic distinction between the two is that the formal organization emphasizes *positions* in terms of authority and functions, whereas the emphasis in informal organization is on *people* and their relationships. It follows that informal organization is not subject to management control in the way that formal organization is.

There are three facts about informal organization that the manager should accept from the outset:

1. The informal organization is inevitable. Management can eliminate any aspect of the formal organization because it is created by management. The informal organization is not created by management, and it cannot be cancelled by management. As long as there are people in an organization, there will be an informal organization.

2. Small groups are the central component of the informal organization, and group membership strongly influences the overall behavior and performance of members. Many sociologists now believe that the social unit (group), rather than the individual, is the basic component of the human organization.

3. Informal organization has both positive and negative consequences. We shall examine the advantages and the

---

[1] Peter M. Blau and W. Richard Scott, *Formal Organizations* (San Francisco: Chandler Publishing Company, 1962), p. 6.

[2] For a complete account of these studies, see F. J. Roethlisberger and W. J. Dickson, *Management and the Worker* (Cambridge, MA: Harvard University Press, 1939).

disadvantages in depth later. To capitalize on the advantages and to minimize the disadvantages, the manager must understand the informal organization and to do this he must understand the groups within it.

Why People Form Groups

When one considers why another human being does anything, the obvious starting point is motivation. Motivation theory has taught us that humans are motivated by things that satisfy their needs. If the formal organization satisfied all the needs of all organizational participants then there would be no informal organization. Informal groups come into being primarily in response to those needs of its members that cannot be fully met in the context of the formal organization alone. The interpersonal contacts within the small group provide some relief from the boredom, monotony, and pressures of the formal organization. The individual in a group is usually surrounded by others who share similar values, thus reinforcing the individual's own value system.

A second reason that people join small groups is the fact that informal status (which may be nothing more than belonging to a distinct little unit which is more or less exclusive) can be accorded by the group.

Third, group membership provides a degree of personal security; the group member knows that he is accepted by his peers as an equal. Group membership permits the individual to express himself before generally sympathetic listeners. The individual gains satisfaction for his recognition, participation, and communication needs. He may even find an outlet for his leadership drives. These important forms of satisfaction are available in the group—usually to a greater degree than the formal organization permits.

Another very important reason for group membership is to secure information. The grapevine is a phenomenon familiar to all organizational participants. Technically, it is the informal communication channel of the organization. Chapter 7 will treat this topic more completely. Suffice it to say here that informal group membership provides the member an inside track on the flow of informal communication in the organization.

The common denominator of all of these reasons for group membership is that they meet specific needs of members that cannot be fully met by the formal organization. Informal groups arise and persist in the organization because they perform desired functions for their members.

Characteristics of Informal Groups

Edwin B. Flippo has suggested that informal groups tend to possess the following characteristics: (1) a tendency to remain small, (2) the satisfaction of group member wants, (3) the development of unofficial leadership, (4) a highly complex structure of relationships, and (5) a tendency toward stability.[3]

The first two of these reasons have already been touched on. Since interpersonal relationships are the essence of informal organization, the informal group must remain small enough so that its individual members can interact frequently. We have also seen that the motivation to form these groups is that they provide a mechanism for members to satisfy needs not satisfied by the formal organization structure.

The use of small group leaders has been studied extensively. Some of the general conclusions about them can be summarized as follows:

1. The leadership role is filled by an individual who possesses the attributes that the group members perceive as being critical for satisfying their needs.
2. The leader embodies the values of the group from which he emerges. He is able to perceive these values, organize them into an intelligible philosophy, and verbalize them to nonmembers.
3. The leader is able to receive and filter communication relevant to the group and effectively communicate the new information to the group. This role can be thought of as an information center.[4]

The informal group leader emerges from within the group because he can serve several functions for it. He serves not only to initiate action and provide direction but to compromise differences of opinion that exist on group-related matters. Furthermore, the group leader serves to communicate values and feelings to nonmembers. Only as long as he is able to perform these functions can he maintain his leadership role.

Another important characteristic of small groups is their tendency to develop a highly complex structure of relationships. In the informal organization, structure is determined by the different status positions that people have. Essentially, there are four status positions:

---

[3] Edwin B. Flippo, *Management: A Behavioral Approach,* 3rd ed. (Boston: Allyn and Bacon, 1978). For an excellent treatment of these and other informal group characteristics, see Chapter 10 of this book.

[4] William G. Scott and Terrence R. Mitchell, *Organization Theory* (Homewood, IL: Richard D. Irwin, Inc., and The Dorsey Press, 1972), p. 97.

1. group leader
2. member of the primary group
3. fringe status
4. out status

Suppose, for example, that we wanted to determine the structure of a group of nine people working in a section of the clinical laboratory. These people are located in a close general area, and there are no artificial barriers, such as walls, to prevent their frequent association with each other. Experience tells us that each person will not associate with each other person with equal frequency. Instead, they will be selective in their association, regularly including some and excluding others.

Using sociometric techniques, which may be nothing more than observation, we can measure this phenomenon, and an accurate picture of the nature of the informal organization of laboratory people can be obtained. (See Figure 6-1.)

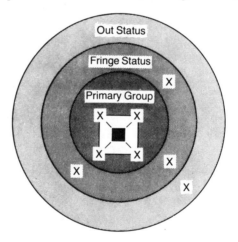

Figure 6-1. A model of informal organization.

The solid square in the center represents the leader of the small group. Clustered around him are four other members of the primary group. Their association is close and is characterized by intense interaction and communication.

The three people in the fringe area are most likely new-comers. They are, in effect, being evaluated by the primary group and may in time become full members. If they are not accepted they will move to out status. In this case, one person is already in out status. Although a part of the informal organization, this person is not accepted by the members of the primary group. Such status can have profound behavioral effects if the person in the out status wants to belong to the primary group. In some cases the rejection is mutual or may even be rejection of the group by the person in out status. In these cases, the person in out status may get along quite well without primary group membership.

The informal organization is not limited to group membership. It also exists as people in the formal organization deal with each other in the accomplishment of work within the context of the formal organization. Figure 6-2 indicates the actual contacts between particular people in the organization. Observe that not all contacts go through formal channels; in some cases certain levels of the organization are bypassed, and in other cases cross-contact is seen from one chain of command to another.

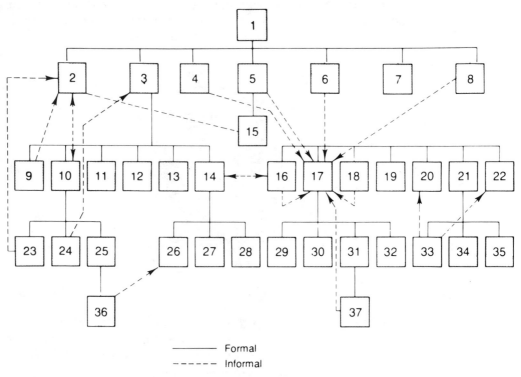

Figure 6-2. A contact chart.

Such charts do not show the reason for the informal relationships, but they do serve the purpose of illustrating the complexity of the informal organization. It is quite possible that a complete understanding of complex organizations cannot be achieved within the present state of the art of organization theory. When the formal organization and the informal organizations are considered together, they may simply be too complex for that understanding.

The final characteristic of the informal group that we should examine is their tendency toward stability. As Keith Davis has suggested, "Although informal organizations are bound by no chart on the wall, they are bound by convention, custom, and culture."[5] To the manager it may appear that the informal organization resists all change. In truth, the informal organization resists only those changes that are interpreted as threats. It takes a great deal of time to establish the strong interpersonal ties that exist among people in the informal organization. Abrupt acts of management can break these ties instantaneously. For this reason, changes that are seen as a threat to established patterns in the informal organization will be resisted.

For example, let us assume that the business office of a hospital has been functioning for some time with a certain physical layout. The informal groups and relationships that have evolved over time are probably deeply entrenched. The manager may decide, however, to rearrange the layout of the business office in the interest of efficiency. The decision could cause the breakup of the patterns of social relations among the office staff and would quite likely be resisted. In many cases, changes of this type are countered by resistance in the form of complaints, work slowdown, reduction in quality, absenteeism, and so on. If management is to influence the acceptance of such change, it must be aware of and understand the dynamics of the informal organization.

POSITIVE ASPECTS OF INFORMAL ORGANIZATION

Complements the Formal Organization

The key benefit of the informal organization is that it blends with the formal organization to generate an operable system for the accomplishment of work. The formal plans and policies of the organization tend to be too inflexible to meet all the needs of a dynamic situation. Thus, the flexible and spontaneous characteristics of the informal organization can be of great advantage if they permit or even encourage deviations in the interest of material contributions toward the organization's objectives.

---

[5] Keith Davis, *Human Behavior at Work*, 5th Edition (New York: McGraw-Hill Book Company, 1977).

Dubin was among the first to recognize the necessary complementarity of the formal and informal organization when he stated, "Informal relations in the organization serve to preserve the organization from the self-destruction that would result from literal obedience to the formal policies, rules, regulations, and procedures."[6]

Provides Necessary Social Values and Stability to Work Groups

Turnover may be caused by a poor matching of person and job or by such pragmatic reasons as a better job or a necessary move. However, research has shown that some resignations occur because the new employee is unable to become a primary member of one or more informal groups. Group membership is a basic means by which employees achieve a sense of belonging and security. If an organization is so cold and impersonal that informal, interpersonal contacts are not encouraged or even, in some cases, permitted, then some new employees may seek employment elsewhere. Of course, informal group membership can be carried to such an extreme that the work place becomes merely a social circle and results in a detrimental effect on work output. Good management can avoid this extreme and provide an atmosphere where workers, through informal relationships, can meet their human needs of acceptance and gregariousness.

Simplifies the Manager's Job

In a very real sense, the informal organization can make things easier for the manager *if he or she remains in control of the situation.* It has been shown that when informal group support is available to the manager he can supervise in a much more general way than when such support is not available. The manager can delegate and decentralize when the informal group is cooperative. Obviously the converse of this is true. The task of the manager is to understand the informal organization and use it to his advantage. Flippo has stated:

> Awareness of the nature and impact of informal organization often leads to better management decisions. Acceptance of the fact that formal relationships will not enable full accomplishment of organiza-

---

[6] Robert Dubin, *Human Relations in Administration* (Englewood Cliffs, NJ: Prentice-Hall, Inc., 1951), p. 68.

tion tasks stimulates management to seek other means of motivation. If most of the work is done informally, the manager will seek to improve his knowledge of the nature of people in general and his subordinates in particular. If he realizes that organization performance can be affected by the granting or withholding of cooperation and enthusiasm, he will seek other means than the formal to develop desirable attitudes.[7]

Provides an Additional Channel of Communication

A well-known benefit of informal organization is that it provides an additional channel of communication for the organization. The grapevine can add to managers' effectiveness if they will study and use it. It can serve to get certain information to employees and can be used to determine employee feelings and attitudes on various issues. The grapevine can cause problems if it is not understood by management. In a very real sense, all of the advantages of the informal organization carry the seeds of trouble. Some of the potential disadvantages are examined in the following section.

NEGATIVE ASPECTS OF INFORMAL ORGANIZATION

Anyone who has had to deal with an informal organization realizes that the advantages outlined above are not always realized—indeed, in many cases the disadvantages far outweigh the potential advantages. The formal organization deals with human behavior as we would like it to occur in the organization, while the informal organization deals with human behavior as it actually occurs.

The most clear-cut disadvantage is that in many situations the individuals and groups that comprise the informal organization can and on occasion do work at cross-purposes with the goals and objectives of the formal organization. It is a basic fact of organizational life that what is good for the employee is not always good for the employer and vice versa. The employee may want to meet the requirements of both his group and his employer, but often these requirements are in conflict. What results is known as role conflict.

Suppose we take the situation of the head nurse as an example. On the one hand, administration's expectations stress her role in the managerial system and the need for decision making and planning and controlling activities in her area of responsibility.

---

[7] Flippo, *Management: A Behavioral Approach,* p. 252.

On the other hand, as a first-line supervisor she often has close ties with the nursing personnel in her unit—her former peers in many cases. Their expectations for her do not necessarily coincide with those coming down from administration. Furthermore, she has many inputs from other head nurses and her own perception of the role to be played. Usually it is not possible to satisfy simultaneously the expectations of two or more participants when compliance with one precludes compliance with the others.

A good bit of this role conflict can be avoided by recognizing that the more compatible the interests, goals, methods, and evaluation systems of the formal and informal organizations can be made, the more productivity and satisfaction can be expected. However, as Keith Davis has pointed out, there will always be differences between the formal and informal organizations' expectations of people.[8]

It should be noted that even the potentially negative impact of conflict should be weighed against its constructive and positive function in fostering creativity and innovation. A relatively conflict-free organization tends to be static. Thus, some conflict should exist as a condition for the generation of fresh ideas.

LIVING WITH THE INFORMAL ORGANIZATION

We have seen that the coexistence of the informal organization within the formal structure is a fact of organizational life. The formal and informal aspects of the organization must be balanced if optimum performance and objective attainment (both for individuals and for the organization) are to be achieved.

If management tries to suppress the informal organization, it creates a destructive situation: the informal organization, in order to protect the employees and to make the work situation acceptable in their view, gains strength to counteract the autocratic administration. The opposing forces clash, and the result is reduced organizational effectiveness.

On the other hand, if the formal organization is too weak to accomplish its objectives, the informal organization can grow in strength; this may lead to such undesirable abuses of power as work restriction, insubordination, disloyalty, and other manifestations of a generally anti-institution attitude.

The optimum situation is one in which the formal organization is strong enough to maintain a unified thrust toward attain-

---

[8] Davis, *Human Behavior at Work.*

ment of its objectives but at the same time permits a well-developed informal organization to maintain group cohesiveness and teamwork; in other words, the ideal is when the informal organization is strong enough to be a positive force, but not so strong as to dominate the formal organization.

A relationship such as the one described above is, at best, difficult to achieve. There are, however, several steps that can be taken to move the organization in the direction of a properly balanced formal and informal relationship. Among them are the following.

1. Management must understand the informal organization, and its actions must convince employees that it understands and accepts the informal organization. For any action taken by management, it is of paramount importance to consider the impact on, and the resultant implications for, the informal organization.

2. Management must, to the maximum extent possible, integrate the interests of the informal organization with those of the formal organization. In doing this, management should attempt to keep actions taken through the formal organization from unnecessarily threatening the informal pattern of relationships.

The informal relationships that exist in any organization are among the more important. They deserve the attention of everyone concerned with the effectiveness of the organization. Recognition of the informal organization reflects the manager's recognition that people in organizations are not mechanistic—they are instead changing, complex, and social beings.

SUMMARY

This chapter on the informal aspects of organization should be viewed as an extension of the previous chapter on the formal aspects of organization. In truth the formal and informal aspects of the organization don't exist as separate areas of concern for the manager because they are so entwined as to be inseparable.

We have defined the informal organization as those relationships and interactions that occur spontaneously out of the activities of members of the organization, but that are not set forth in the formal structure. The astute manager will recognize three key facts about the informal organization:

1. It is inevitable.

2. Small groups are the heart of the informal organization.

3. The informal organization has both positive and negative consequences.

To understand fully the formal organization, the manager must understand small groups and their behavior patterns. Small groups form in the work setting for several reasons, among them: needs of the group members that are not satisfied by the formal organization, informal status, security, and to secure information.

Although the existence of the informal organization presents some problems for the manager, such as the fact that often the informal organization may work at cross purposes with the formal organization, it does have certain advantages. It can complement the formal organization, especially where too much inflexibility is built into the formal structure. It may provide very important social values and stability to work groups. In fact, it can simplify the manager's job *if he or she remains in control of the situation.*

The effective manager recognizes the existence of *both* formal and informal aspects of the organization and uses both to advantage.

Directing: The Interpersonal Aspect of Management

SEVEN

**MAY 1ST
3:40 P.M.**

The Surgeon who had operated on Luther Fillerey caught up with the Director of Nursing just as she was leaving the hospital to go to a meeting of other local Nursing Directors.

"Listen," she said, a little breathless from her long run down the corridor, "I've been meaning to talk to you for some time now about the way your people handled this situation with Luther Fillerey!"

The Director of Nursing looked at the Surgeon, a woman whom she thought was highly skilled as a surgeon but entirely too abrasive in her relationships with other people at Memorial Hospital, and responded, "What do you mean?"

"I mean the Fillereys have been my friends for years, and I left strict orders that if there was *any* change in his condition that I was to be called—no matter when!"

The Director looked at the Surgeon sternly and replied, "Doctor, you know very well that the usual policy is to call the Chief Resident when a problem occurs after 9:00 p.m."

"I know that," she retorted, "but I left specific instructions with your Head Nurse that I was to be called in this case."

The Director folded her arms and replied, "I don't know who is at fault here. My nurses always try to carry out doctors' orders for their patients—even when they lie outside the usual hospital policy. I'll look into the matter and get back to you."

"I just want you to know that I'm very disturbed by this incident. If you can't get your nurses to follow directions, you should find some who can!" With that, the Surgeon wheeled around and went on to make her afternoon rounds in the hospital.

The Director of Nursing got into her car and left for the meeting. As she drove she thought, "Somebody should have called her, I suppose. The day shift probably forgot to pass the word along to the night shift people—anyway, it isn't the usual policy to call anyone but the Chief Resident at that time of night. That delay is going to make me late for this meeting. It's already four o'clock."

INTRODUCTION

At some point in the management process there has to be a means for the manager to indicate to the managed what he or she wants done. Once plans have been made and an organizational structure has been created to put them into effect, the next logical function of management is to stimulate the effort needed to perform the required work. When viewed as parts of the whole management process, planning and organizing can be considered as preparatory managerial functions. As we shall see, the purpose of controlling is to find out whether or not objectives are being met. Thus, directing and coordinating (as we will see in Chapter 8) are the connecting and actuating links between these functions. The importance of directing is contained in one thought—it is the managerial function that initiates action.

In general, directing means the issuance of orders, assignments, and instructions that permit the subordinate to understand what is expected of him, and the guidance and overseeing of the subordinate so that he can contribute effectively and efficiently to the attainment of organizational objectives.

In many ways, directing is the most complex of the management functions. This is true mainly because the directing function is the interpersonal aspect of managing. The manager must deal with people as individuals and as group members. He or she soon learns that people do not automatically take as their own the objectives of the organization.

THE HUMAN FACTOR

Managers have been skilled in using the material factors of production for a long time. A great deal of information and knowledge about how best to utilize material factors has been generated by economists, engineers, and financiers. In contrast, the human

135

factor has been far less understood and far less effectively utilized as a factor of production. Although much is *not* known, contemporary theory and research have a great deal to say about why people behave the way they do in organizations.

If one analyzes what has been discovered about the nature of human beings, a number of important facts present themselves. Among them:

1. *There is no such thing as the average human being.* People differ in terms of basic mental abilities, personality, interests, level of aspiration, energy, education, experience, and so on. From the day of his birth, each person is unique. For the rest of his life, the people, things, and events with which he comes in contact make him even more different because they constitute a part of his experience. Attempts to take some kind of arithmetical average of people will fail, and attempts to deal with individuals as if they represented some hypothetical average will fail. Many managers are unsuccessful because they take a standard, across-the-board way of relating to other people in almost every situation. This tendency is exhibited by many managers because it greatly simplifies their job, at least as they view it.

2. *Human beings work to satisfy their own needs.* All normal human behavior is caused by a person's need structure. Workers have a perception of their needs which often differs from what management thinks they have. Furthermore, not all workers perceive their needs in the same way. An even more complex factor is that as an individual grows older, his perception of his own needs changes. These facts make it very difficult for a manager, especially one who supervises a large number of people, to create an environment in which workers can satisfy their needs. After all, the manager only thinks he or she knows what their needs are. This is made even more complex by the fact that needs are so different from one worker to another and by the fact that the needs of an individual are constantly changing. Yet the manager must keep in mind that getting a worker to carry out a directive is caused behavior. Since this behavior is caused by the employee's attempt to satisfy some need, the manager has but two ways to get the employee to carry out a directive. He or she can make the employee see that a desired action will increase his need fulfillment, or the manager can convince the employee that he or she must carry out the directive to avoid a decreased need fulfillment.

What this means is that management's ability to direct successfully depends almost entirely on the fact that, from the employee's point of view, management controls the means by which the employee can meet many of his or her needs.

We shall return to this matter of need fulfillment in a later section when the topic is motivation, because need satisfaction is at the heart of motivation.

3. *Human beings respond to leadership.* There is a great deal of evidence that this is true. Yet the reasons why it is true are not well understood. It is clear that a leader is followed if he or she can help the followers meet their needs as they see them. It is important for the manager to take advantage of this part of human nature in the work place. Leadership is not something that can be taught in its entirety. However, certain techniques and procedures have been developed that can assist the manager in the leadership role. Leadership as a part of the directing function of management will be dealt with at length in a later section.

KEYS TO SUCCESSFUL DIRECTING

If one generalization about the directing function can be made, it is this: Success in directing others depends more on the *attitude* of the manager toward the subordinate than on any other single factor. This is true because the manager's attitude toward subordinates dictates his approach to directing their activities.

For example, one manager may be convinced that most human beings have an inherent dislike of work and seek to avoid it. Another may believe that they do not inherently dislike work and that they in fact want to work as a part of their basic nature. These opposing attitudes will result in one manager using coercion to get work done while another relies to a larger extent on the workers' own initiative. Most managers probably lie somewhere in between these two attitudes, but the point is that what the manager believes about his subordinates affects the methods he uses in directing them; this in turn determines his success in the effort.

Another dichotomous attitude is that some managers feel very strongly that most human beings prefer to be directed; others believe that subordinates want to exercise their own initiatives and imaginations in seeking creative solutions to work problems. Clearly, these opposing attitudes will yield different styles of management and probably different results.

Management authorities, in observing such opposing attitudes in managers, have labeled them "traditional" and "modern." The evidence is all around us that most people, given the chance for meaningful work, relish it and seek to exercise initiative, seek responsibility, and seek to display ingenuity and creativity in their approach to work. These concepts have come to be called the modern, or the human relations, approach to management.

Successful directing, based on the modern attitudes described above, depends largely on the maturity of the manager and the subordinates. Often, managers are inclined not to relinquish tight control over the activities of their subordinates because they believe that workers lack the maturity for self-control. This position defines maturity in mutually exclusive terms as a state of existence that an employee either does or does not possess. In reality, maturity is more accurately defined as a goal rather than as something static. Maturity is developed, and the rate at which it develops depends on environmental factors that allow and encourage it to grow in the individual.

In applying the modern approach to directing subordinates, the manager's central task is to show the subordinate that his objectives and the objectives of the health services organization are essentially compatible. It is doubtful whether organizational objectives can be identical to those of the individual. However, the similarity is often greater than some managers assume. Even when the worker's objectives are not identical to those of the health services organization, it does not mean that they must be mutually exclusive.

THE CENTRAL TASK IN DIRECTING: ISSUING ORDERS

No matter what approach a manager takes to directing his subordinates, at some point he has to indicate what he wants done. The order is the technical means through which a subordinate understands what is to be done.

In health services organizations, as in other enterprises, the right to give orders, from a purely legal point of view, stems from a contract involving the services of subordinates. The organization employs the individual to perform certain duties, undertakes to explain what is needed through its managers, and pays the employee for his services. The employee undertakes the specified activities and receives his remuneration for doing so. This legalistic explanation does not tell the whole story.

Ideally, there should be understanding and acceptance of the order by the subordinate. To facilitate this there are certain characteristics of good orders which managers should be aware of.

1. The order should be clear, concise, and consistent. The purpose is to give sufficient information to ensure understanding.

2. Orders should be based on obvious demands of particular situations. If the order conforms to the requirements of a particular situation, it seems logical to the subordinate and not just an arbitrary whim of the manager.

3. The tone of the order is important. If the subordinate is to accept the order fully, he must feel that the manager is doing his job by pointing out something that needs to be done and not merely exercising his power over the subordinate. The manner in which the manager delivers the order has a great deal to do with its acceptance by the subordinate.

4. Whenever possible, the reason for the order should be given. A subordinate will accept an order more readily if he understands the need for it. There are occasions when lack of information on the part of the manager or scarcity of time prohibits this; however, this should be the exception and not the rule.

DELEGATION AS A MEANS OF DIRECTING

Delegation of authority is a more general form of directing than issuance of orders. In delegation, the manager usually gives a subordinate authority to act in a certain area of activity by means of a general statement. Delegation is less exact than an order since it often merely states that the subordinate is authorized to carry out assigned duties. The degree of detail in a grant of authority is usually determined by how detailed the work assignment is. Delegation is more often the means by which one manager directs the activities of a subordinate manager than for a manager to direct a worker. However, in situations involving professionals or highly trained technical people, the manager may use delegation as a means of avoiding too many specific orders.

MOTIVATIONAL ASPECTS OF THE DIRECTING FUNCTION

Picture for a moment a manager and two employees. The manager issues an order to both employees. One employee receives the order and carries it out. He performs the assignment to the best of his ability as soon as his schedule permits. He does not complain that he has been assigned the task unfairly; he questions the assignment only to the point necessary for him to completely understand it, and he uses whatever abilities and skills he has to make certain the assignment is properly carried out. The other employee receives the same order. He complains that the assignment should not be his. He tells the manager that he won't have time to carry out the task anytime soon. After considerable "pushing" by the manager, the employee finally carries out the assignment, but only in a very halfhearted and minimal way. The differences between the two situations, both in the way the assignment is performed and the feelings of the manager as well as the employees, are the differences motivation makes and account for its importance.

All other things being equal, we can assume that the first employee is more highly motivated than the second. Perhaps the most difficult task managers in an organization face is that of motivating employees—managerial and nonmanagerial alike—to perform the work assigned to them in a manner that meets or exceeds expected standards.

Many methods have been used to encourage employees to put forth their best efforts. The existence of so many approaches to motivation, along with the fact that they have not been very successful, suggest the complexity of the problem of motivation.

Motivation Defined

Motivation is not a simple concept. The central thread that runs through the current thinking on motivation is that motivated behavior is *goal-directed* behavior. Figure 7-1 illustrates this. The diagram shows that the process begins with a need that must be satisfied by the individual who feels it. This results in activity and/or behavior that is intended to satisfy the need (goal-directed behavior). It may be blocked, which results in frustration for the individual. The cyclical nature of the motivational process is shown in the diagram by the fact that when a need is satisfied (a goal is achieved), the individual redefines his or her needs in light of what

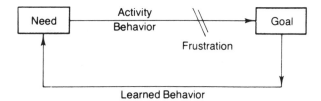

Figure 7-1. The process of motivation.

he or she has learned; this, added to previously unsatisfied needs, initiates another round of the process. We are concerned with motivating workers to achieve higher levels of productivity, but human behavior in general is motivated by this need-satisfying process. Needing power, one person runs for political office; wanting status, another buys his way into a certain country club; fearing threats to his self-esteem, another avoids situations in which his intellectual competence might be compromised. And so it goes through life and work—a need is felt, goal-directed behavior alleviates the need, and new or redefined needs take its place.

Thus motivation refers to the way in which needs (urges, aspirations, desires) control, direct, or explain the behavior of human beings.

Motivation Theories

The complexity of motivating human behavior is perhaps best illustrated in the diversity of theoretical underpinnings that have been developed to explain it. Several of the most important theories are described in this section. These theories can be divided into two broad categories: (1) content theories and (2) process theories.[1]

The content theories attempt to identify specifically what it is within the individual or within his environment that initiates, sustains, and eventually terminates his behavior. The process theories are intended to explain how behavior is initiated, sustained, or terminated. The process theories define the variables that explain motivated behavior and then try to show how the variables interact with and influence each other to produce certain behavioral patterns within people. Examples of the theoretical development of motivation in both areas are cited below.

---

[1] John P. Campbell, Marvin D. Dunnette, Edward E. Lawler, III, and Karl E. Weick, Jr., *Managerial Behavior, Performance, and Effectiveness* (New York: McGraw-Hill Book Company, 1970), p. 341.

Content
Theories

CLASSICAL THEORY.   The most basic example of a content theory can be traced back to the work of Frederick W. Taylor in the early 1900's.[2] His reasoning was straightforward: Make it possible for men to earn more by producing more and they will. You may remember that Taylor was able to increase the average number of tons of iron ingots handled by each man per day at Bethlehem Steel from 12 ½ to 47 ½. The average cost of handling a tone was reduced from 9.2¢ to 3.9¢, and at the same time, the workers' average daily earnings went from $1.15 to $1.85. These are impressive statistics, and comparable improvements in productivity would be welcomed in any health services organization today. Unfortunately, the straightforward power of money as a motivator is not so great today. In fact, it never fully explained motivation for all people. To believe it did, or does, would mean ignoring all those who have forsaken financial security for the betterment of the human condition. Money can motivate some people to some extent, but it is not the whole answer to motivation—it is not the only need that people work to satisfy.

HIERARCHY OF NEEDS.   Abraham H. Maslow is the author of one of the most widely known content theories of motivation. Maslow, a psychologist, stressed two fundamental premises in his theory of motivation:

1. Man is a wanting animal whose needs depend on what he already has. Only needs not yet satisfied can influence behavior; an adequately fulfilled need is not a motivator.
2. Man's needs are arranged in a heirarchy of importance. Once a particular need is fulfilled, another emerges and demands fulfillment.

Maslow's need theory, first publicized in the early 1940's, stressed a heirarchy with certain "higher" needs becoming dominant after other "lower" needs were satisfied.[3] Figure 7-2 illustrates the hierarchy. Each need category is briefly described below:

1. *Physiological needs.* This category consists of the basic survival needs for food, water, sex, and so on.

---

[2] Frederick W. Taylor, *Scientific Management* (New York: Harper and Row, Publishers, 1919).
[3] Abraham H. Maslow, "A Theory of Human Motivation," *Psychological Review,* July 1943, pp. 370-396.

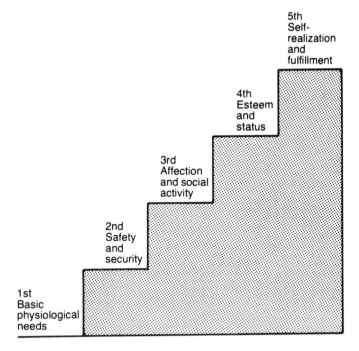

Figure 7-2. Hierarchy of human needs.

2. *Safety and security needs.* Once the survival needs are met, attention can be turned to ensuring continued survival by protecting oneself against physical harm and deprivation.

3. *Affection and social activity needs.* This third level of needs is related to the social and gregarious nature of humans. This is something of a breaking point in the hierarchy in that it begins to get away from the physical or quasiphysical needs of the first two levels. These needs exhibit themselves in people's need for association or companionship with others, for belonging to groups, and for giving and receiving friendship and affection.

4. *Esteem and status needs.* These are the needs for self-respect or self-esteem, which come from an awareness of one's importance to others. One's status, or level of importance relating to others, is an important need in this category.

5. *Self-actualization needs.* This highest level of human needs includes the need to achieve the fullest development of one's potential. It exhibits itself in the need to be creative and to have the opportunity for self-expression.

These categories of needs can be separated for purposes of analysis or discussion, but in truth they are interacting together within the individual. The lower level needs are never completely satisfied—they recur from time to time. The needs for esteem and self-actualization are such that once they become important to a person he seeks indefinitely for more satisfaction of them. In fact, people can never fully satisfy all of their needs. Even if all those an individual has today could somehow be satisfied, the person would generate new ones.

The need hierarchy model essentially says that satisfied needs are no longer strongly motivating. People are motivated by what they are seeking much more than by what they already have.

Figure 7-3 shows the relative mix of needs for an individual as he develops over time. It shows progressive changes and the relative importance, number, and variety of needs. The diagram shows that the peak of a "lower" level need must be passed before a "higher" level need becomes dominant.

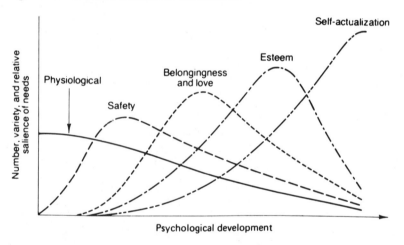

Figure 7-3. Relative importance of needs as motivators.

From James H. Donnelly, Jr., James L. Gibson, and John M. Ivancevich, *Fundamentals of Management: Functions, Behavior, Models,* 3rd ed. (Dallas, Tex.: Business Publications, 1978), p. 192. © 1978 by Business Publications, Inc.

The application of this theory in the work place necessitates a realization that human beings have a variety of needs that will motivate them. The management task becomes one of developing situations in the work place that permit the employee to satisfy one of his or her needs.

People are not always able to satisfy their needs, and the manager should know what kinds of behavior this elicits. In general, frustration occurs when one is blocked from meeting one or more of his needs. It is important for the manager to recognize and understand frustration as it affects his subordinates and himself. Frustration may occur when an employee has a strong need for esteem but his job is such that he cannot satisfy this need. It is up to management to restructure the job so that such needs can be met. There is no job in the health services organization that is not in some way related to patient care. The employee who is scrubbing floors may not realize this because the relationship has not been explained to him. However, when such an employee realizes that he is not merely scrubbing floors but, rather, helping to provide the sanitary environment so necessary for good patient care, then the chance that he can fulfill his needs for feeling self-respect and esteem in his work is greatly improved.

Frustration is a *feeling* rather than a *fact.* It is a feeling that arises when one encounters certain kinds of blocks to fulfilling his needs. These feelings arise when the blocks seem insurmountable and when failure to surmount them threatens one's personal well-being.

When frustration occurs for an individual, he gets aggressive. If the person is optimistic about his ability to reach his goal (or satisfy a particular need by reaching his goal), he gets aggressive outwardly. He attacks the obstacle. If he is pessimistic about his own ability, he gets aggressive inwardly. He attacks himself. This is a key idea because it allows the perceptive manager to better understand both herself and her frustrations and those of her subordinates.

For example, suppose a nurse needs a feeling of accomplishment in her work. For some reason (usually to satisfy some need of her own), a physician constantly belittles the nurse and her work. The result is a block put in the path to her satisfaction of the need for esteem, and frustration follows. The nurse may react by being aggressive to the physician—by sharp words to her or to other people about her. On the other hand, she may attack herself and her own abilities and end up feeling less valuable and capable than she really is.

The manner in which the frustrated person reacts can range from a scowl to an overt physical attack. This reaction is influenced by the personality of the frustrated individual. The reaction may not be chosen consciously but may be the product of unconscious learning. Many of these unconscious reactions to the tensions created by frustrations are called defense mechanisms. Some of the most common defense mechanisms are as follows:

1. *Withdrawal.* One way to avoid frustration is to withdraw or avoid frustrating situations. This may result in physically leaving the scene, but more likely will result in apathy.

2. *Displacement.* Often it is not possible to be aggressive toward the person who is causing the frustration (a superior for example), so the aggression is directed toward another person—a spouse or a child or a peer.

3. *Compensation.* Sometimes a person goes overboard in one area of activity to make up for deficiencies in another area.

4. *Repression.* Sometimes a person can repress a frustrating situation by losing awareness of it since it would cause frustration if allowed to remain at the conscious level of the mind.

5. *Regression.* Some people revert to childlike behavior in their attempt to avoid an unpleasant reality. This often exhibits itself as horseplay in the work place.

6. *Rationalization.* People are often able to convince themselves that a reason for not being able to satisfy a need lies outside themselves. This is often less ego-deflating than the real reason. For example, a medical technologist may explain poor lab work by blaming obsolete equipment rather than some deficiency of his own.

TWO-FACTOR THEORY.   In 1959, Herzberg, Mausner, and Snyderman reported research findings suggesting that people have two sets of needs: their need as animals to avoid pain and their needs as humans to grow psychologically. These findings led them to advance a "dual factor" theory of motivation.[4]

Whereas previous theories of motivation were based on causal inferences of the theories and deduction from their own insights and experience, the dual-factor theory of motivation was inferred from a study of need satisfactions and the reported motivational effects of these satisfactions on 200 engineers and accountants. The subjects were first requested to recall a time when they had felt exceptionally good about their jobs. The investigators sought, by further questioning, to determine the reasons for their feelings of satisfaction and whether these feelings had affected their performance, their personal relationships, and their well-being. Finally, the sequence of events that served to return the workers' attitudes to "normal" was elicited.

In a second set of interviews, the same subjects were asked to describe incidents in which their feelings about their jobs were exceptionally negative—cases in which their negative feelings were related to some event on the job. Herzberg and his associates

---

[4] Frederick Herzberg, Bernard Mausner, and Barbara Snyderman, *The Motivation to Work,* 2nd ed. (New York: John Wiley and Sons, Inc., 1959).

concluded from their interview findings that job satisfaction consisted of two separate independent dimensions.[5]

1. There are some conditions of the job which, when absent, operate primarily to dissatisfy employees. However, the presence of these conditions does not build strong motivation to contribute more effort. Herzberg called these factors *maintenance* factors since they are necessary to maintain a reasonable level of satisfaction. He also noted that many of these factors have often been perceived by managers as motivators, but that they are, in fact, more potent as dissatisfiers when they are absent. He concluded that there were ten maintenance factors, namely:
   (a) organization policy and administration
   (b) technical supervision
   (c) interpersonal relations with supervisor
   (d) interpersonal relations with peers
   (e) interpersonal relations with subordinates
   (f) salary
   (g) job security
   (h) personal life
   (i) work conditions
   (j) status

2. There are other job conditions which, if present, operate to build high levels of motivation and job satisfaction. However, if these conditions are not present, they do not prove highly dissatisfying. Herzberg described six of these factors as motivational factors or satisfiers:
   (a) achievement
   (b) recognition
   (c) advancement
   (d) the work itself
   (e) the possibility of growth
   (f) responsibility

When the Herzberg and Maslow models are compared, it can be seen that they both emphasize the same set of relationships. Both are content theories in that they look at *what* motivates human behavior. Maslow looked at the human needs of the individual while Herzberg focused on how the job conditions affect the individual's basic needs. Figure 7-4 illustrates this.

---

[5] This discussion is adapted from James H. Donnelly, Jr., James L. Gibson, and John M. Ivancevich, *Fundamentals of Management: Functions, Behavior, Models* (Dallas: Business Publications, Inc., 1978), pp. 188-192.

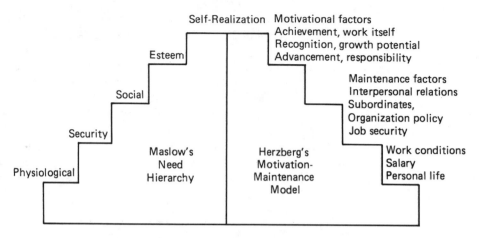

Figure 7-4. A comparison of the Maslow and Herzberg models.

From James H. Donnelly, Jr., James L. Gibson, and John M. Ivancevich, *Fundamentals of Management: Functions, Behavior, Models,* 3rd ed. (Dallas, Tex.: Business Publications, 1978), p. 192. © 1978 by Business Publications, Inc.

The basic advance of Herzberg's theory of motivation over the Maslow model of need-priority is that it shows the distinction between maintenance and motivational factors. Of importance for the application of motivation theory in the work place, Herzberg also shows that motivation derives mostly from the work itself.

Process Theory

PREFERENCE-EXPECTATION THEORY.   We have looked at three content theories. Victor H. Vroom has developed a motivational model, which enlarges the concepts of Maslow and Herzberg and which can be considered a process theory.[6] His preference-expectation theory is more an explanation of the motivation phenomenon than it is a description of what motivates (the content theories we have looked at). Vroom's theory explains how two variables (preference and expectation) work to determine motivation. Preference, in Vroom's model, refers to the possible outcomes that an individual might experience as the result of any activity. If, for example, a clerk in the business office files more documents than other clerks she may receive higher pay, get a promotion, impress her supervisor, or make her co-workers jealous. Many other outcomes are possible—including the possibility that nothing will happen. The clerk clearly has a preference. The other part of the Vroom model is expectancy. This is the individual's expectation that a desired

---

[6] Victor H. Vroom, *Work and Motivation* (New York: John Wiley and Sons, 1964).

outcome will actually happen. An individual with a preference for an outcome must also feel that he can achieve the outcome by doing certain things. The importance of the Vroom model is that it emphasizes the fact that motivation as a process is an individual thing. It depends upon the individual having a specific, preferred outcome coupled with a belief or expectation that certain activities or behavior will bring about the desired outcome.

Keith Davis has suggested that managers, by utilizing expectancy theory wisely, can increase employee motivation in a rather straightforward way:

> First, we can increase the positive value of outcomes through such means as better communication about their values and actually increasing them (i.e., increasing rewards). Second, we may increase the expectancy that the work really will lead to the desired outcome, that is, we can strengthen the connection between the work and the outcome. We may do this through improved communication, or we may increase the actual probabilities of the outcome. Since expectancy depends entirely on the employee's view of the connection between work and outcome, often a simple, straightforward incentive is more motivating than a complex one. The complex one may provide so much uncertainty that the employee does not sufficiently connect effort with outcome. The simple incentive, on the other hand, provides a workable path that employees can see and understand; therefore, its expectancy is higher.[7]

We have looked at four motivational theories. All are different, yet all are related. The common thread is that motivated behavior is goal-directed. For Taylor the goal was simple—money. Maslow suggested a range of needs that all human beings share and that exist in a hierarchy. Herzberg's two-factor theory develops a distinction between maintenance factors (necessary to avoid dissatisfaction) and motivational factors (the needs by which workers can be motivated). Vroom suggests a way to understand the motivational process: individual preference as to outcomes for his activities and behavior coupled with his expectation that desired outcomes can be achieved.

The Application of Motivation Theory

The present state of the art of motivation theory does not permit us to say with unassailable conviction *what* motivates people nor *how* the phenomenon takes place. The theories are constantly chal-

---

[7] Keith Davis, *Human Behavior at Work, 5th Edition* (New York: McGraw-Hill Book Company, 1977), p. 61.

lenged, expanded, and sometimes discarded. Yet the manager in the health services organization is faced with the day-to-day operational necessity to motivate employees.

There is a growing body of sound empirical evidence that the best motivator is a *challenging job* that allows a feeling of achievement, responsibility, growth, advancement, the enjoyment of the work itself, and earned recognition. This is especially true with professional and high-skill-level workers. The author's own research with registered nurses supports this statement.

A question that concerns many managers is why employees seem so preoccupied with concerns about money and factors that are peripheral to the job (including such things as rules, titles, and their physical surroundings) if these are not the things that really motivate them. The answer is that these are tangible things that easily occur to all of us. The higher order psychological and sociological needs that people have are not as readily understood by the manager or his subordinates. Workers strike out at those things that are obvious, when in truth there are more subtle needs that they are often unable to understand or verbalize. One of the great challenges in motivation is developing in managers the ability to help their subordinates really understand their needs and to help satisfy them within the organization. This is a tremendously complex task for the manager in view of the fact that each employee has a different set of needs and that the needs of each individual are constantly changing.

Even in view of the difficulties associated with motivation, there are some things the manager can do to facilitate motivation of his or her subordinates:

1. *Determine clearly the objectives and purposes of the work to be done.* To motivate, one must first know what he is trying to motivate someone to do. This sounds simple, but it is a step that is often overlooked by managers.

2. *The manager must empathize with his subordinates.* He must see a situation as the employee sees it and feel about it as the employee feels about it. Unless the manager does this, his motivation efforts are going to remain chance affairs probably based on money, since it is the traditional motivator. A significant part of following through this step is to try to help the employee fully understand his needs and wants.

3. *The manager must communicate with his employees.* He may have determined the best motivators to use with a particular employee or group of employees, but unless he can communicate an understanding of what he is doing to the employee,

he will not motivate him. Too often, bright managers who develop excellent ideas are unable to get them across. The manager who is certain that he is communicating full understanding to his employees should reconsider, because communicating effectively is among the most difficult of all management tasks.

4. *The manager must integrate the needs and wants of the employee with the interests of the health services organization.* The organization, as an enterprise, has certain goals and objectives. The employee has his own objectives as determined by his needs. These objectives are not the same. The degree of success of the manager will be largely determined by how well he can integrate the objectives of the employee with those of the organization.

5. *The manager must remove obstructions between the employee and the work to be done.* Effective motivation cannot occur until such obstructions as lack of training, poor equipment and facilities, and working conditions that make it difficult for the employee to do his work have been removed.

6. *The manager must develop teamwork among his subordinates.* He does this by integrating each employee's needs-satisfaction with that of the other employees so that there is a coordinated group effort. This means that it may not be possible to do things that the manager has decided will motivate a certain employee if the effect on several other employees will be negative. He must think of his employees as a group and do what is best for the entire group. However, through careful thought and planning, the manager can do a great deal of individual employee motivation, which will make the group as a whole more effective.

LEADERSHIP AS A PART OF THE DIRECTING FUNCTION

Leadership is a basic and important part of management. Yet it is an ephemeral and elusive concept. It can be defined, at least in the context of the way it functions in health services organizations, as *the accomplishment of organizational objectives as the result of interpersonal relationships between the leader and those he or she leads.* In some ways this definition is similar to the definition of management itself. The two concepts, however, are not really the same. A manager must plan and organize, but a leader must simply get others to follow. The fact that a leader can get others to follow him is no guarantee that he will be a good manager. A strong leader, who is weak in planning or some other managerial activity, may be able to get people going, but he may not take them in directions that serve the organization's objectives. So good leadership ability does not mean the same thing as good managerial ability. It is true, however, that leadership ability is of great value to a manager and that usually a good manager possesses leadership ability. The point is that they are not the same thing.

The Nature of Leadership

Leadership is the ability to inspire and influence others to contribute to the attainment of objectives. This is obviously necessary for getting work done through and by others—which is the manager's task. Traditionally, success in leadership was thought to be dependent on personal traits of the leader. More recently, it has been shown that successful leadership is the result of the interaction between the leader and his subordinates in a particular organizational situation. The different concepts of leadership that have been developed focus around these two broad theoretical approaches: (1) the trait theory and (2) the situational theory.

Until the middle 1940's, most theories of leadership centered around traits possessed by successful leaders. The traits thought to be necessary included such things as objectivity, judgment, initiative, dependability, decisiveness, honesty, drive, and so on. For several reasons, it is not possible to explain leadership fully in terms of personal traits. The chief reason is that the search of social scientists for universal traits in leaders has been unsuccessful. It has not been possible so far to isolate and identify specific traits that are common to all leaders. Furthermore, the trait theory fails to consider the influence of situational factors in leadership. Personal traits are only one part of the whole environment of leadership. Though a certain trait exists, it willl not become active until a certain group in a certain situation calls for it. This means that there is no sure connection between traits and leadership acts.

For these reasons, as well as others, the more modern theories of leadership take the situationist approach and emphasize the existence of leadership roles and skills that are evoked by situations or contexts. Of course, a purely situational view of leadership fails to take into account that leadership is a complex process in which the traits of the leader do play a part.

What these considerations mean is that both the trait and the situational theories have added to our understanding of leadership, although neither has fully explained it. It is clear that leadership ability is influenced by personal traits of the leader, but successful leadership also depends upon the followers, the goals and objectives of all concerned, and the environment in which leadership is practiced. The conclusion to be drawn from this approach is that a single pattern of leadership behavior used without discretion is not likely to be successful in a wide variety of managerial situations. Thus the successful leader is not a blind follower of particular leadership methods; he chooses the method that he considers most appropriate for a given situation. He reaches his choice by considering the overall situation, especially the people he wishes to lead and what effect his actions will have on them. While it is true that no single pattern of leadership behavior will work in every situation, the manager should develop a style that provides him an overall framework in which to practice leadership.

Leadership Style

There are a number of styles of leadership that have been identified. As usual, those that occupy extreme positions have received the most attention. For example, most authorities dichotomize leadership styles as either autocratic or democratic. They may use different terms such as "participative leadership" or the "human relations approach to leadership" to describe democratic leadership and the "scientific-management approach to leadership" to describe autocratic leadership, but the idea is the same. The danger in dichotomizing leadership styles in this way is that we build up stereotypes of each style. These stereotypes mainly involve the attitude of the leader to the subordinates. But as we have seen, leadership involves much more than the kind of interpersonal relationship between superior and subordinate. With so many factors involved, it seems highly unlikely that leadership styles can be realistically classified into one of two classifications: autocratic or democratic. Instead, the relationship between superior and subordinate follows a continuum of leadership behavior, as seen in Figure 7-5. Let's consider each of these seven gradations of leadership behavior:[8]

---

[8] Adapted from Robert Tannenbaum and Warren H. Schmidt, "How to Choose a Leadership Pattern," *Harvard Business Review,* March-April 1958. (Copyright 1958 by the President and Fellows of Harvard College; all rights reserved.)

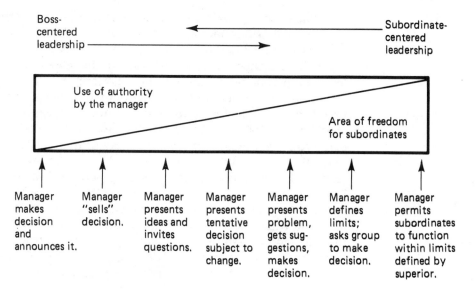

Figure 7-5. Continuum of leadership behavior.

SOURCE: Robert Tannenbaum and Warren H. Schmidt, "How to Choose a Leadership Pattern," *Harvard Business Review,* Vol. 34 (March-April, 1958), p. 96. (Copyright © 1958 by the President and Fellows of Harvard College; all rights reserved).

1. *Manager Makes Decision and Announces It.* This form of leadership represents the most autocratic form; i.e., there is no chance for the subordinate to express his thoughts either in the formulation or the solution of the problem. The superior formulates the problem, solves it, and announces his decision. Coercion, to ensure the execution of the decision, is not necessarily implied since subordinates may be willing to follow such directions.

2. *Manager "Sells" Decision.* At this stage the manager recognizes the feelings of subordinates and the possibility that there might be resistance to his decision. Consequently, he attempts to persuade them to recognize the merits of his decision. However, the manager is still in control of all phases of the decision-making process.

3. *Manager Presents Ideas and Invites Questions.* The third form of leadership behavior marks the beginning of a degree of participation on the part of subordinates—at least they are being asked to express their ideas. However, the manager has in his own mind made the decision. Nonetheless, the presentation of his ideas to subordinates with the opportunity to express themselves opens up the possibility that the decision may be modified.

4. *Manager Presents a Tentative Decision Subject to Change.* Here, at the midpoint of the range of leadership styles, there is definite participation on the part of subordinates in shaping a final decision. Although the manager's decision is tentative, he still defines the problem and works out the initial solution.

5. *Manager Presents Problem, Gets Suggestions, Makes Decision.* This is the first time the manager comes to the group without having at least a tentative solution to the problem; however, he still defines the problem in general terms. Consultation with the group prior to making a tentative decision increases the number of possible solutions.

6. *Manager Defines Limits, Asks Group to Make Decision.* Up to this point the decision is made by the manager with varying degrees of participation on the part of subordinates in influencing his decision; this is the first time that the group makes the decision. However, the manager still states the problem and the limits within which the decision must be made. Usually these limits are expressed in terms of either cost or time, or both.

7. *Manager Permits Subordinates to Function within Limits Defined by Superior.* The last stage of managerial behavior on the scale represents the maximum degree of subordinate participation within formal organizations. The manager, himself usually a subordinate, is limited in the extent to which he may permit participation by the limits of authority granted to him. The greatest degree of subordinate participation is possible within the framework of a Functional-Teamwork or Task-Force type of operation. Even here, the objectives of the organization are stated by higher authority, but subordinates may define and solve problems consistent with the attainment of the objectives of the health services organization.

Selecting An Appropriate Leadership Style

The continuum of leadership styles, therefore, ranges from the completely authoritarian situation with no subordinate participation, to a maximum degree of democratic leadership, enabling the subordinate to participate in all phases of the decision-making process. This concept is a realistic view of the leadership styles available to the manager. The problem then becomes one of selecting the style that is most appropriate.

A number of considerations must be taken into account when selecting one's own style. The following discussion will examine three of the most important and should serve to illustrate that the best leadership style depends on a number of factors and the style that is best in one situation may not be best in another.

THE ORGANIZATIONAL ENVIRONMENT.   Generally, as an organization becomes larger and more complex, leadership styles become more authoritarian in nature. There is a positive relationship, evidenced by the presence of organizational charts, job descriptions, and other means of formal control, between the size of organizations and the formalization of organization structure and relationships. Larger organizations also tend to rely more heavily upon written rather than oral communications, a condition that tends to restrict leadership to more formal, authoritarian styles. Obviously, the structure of an organization provides the technical apparatus through which leadership is made effective or ineffective and thereby has a great deal to do with leadership style.

In organizations such as those delivering modern health services, a great many departments and work units must work cooperatively in meeting their objective of providing high quality care. This requires a high degree of interaction between members of the organization (both between various departments and within individual departments). Managers in these organizations should, therefore, use leadership styles of a more participative, informal nature whenever possible.

THE PERSONALITIES OF ORGANIZATION MEMBERS.   It has been shown in a number of studies that leadership styles are directly affected by the personalities and expectations of subordinates. Subordinates who do not expect participation and who are dependent upon others for motivation react best to authoritarian styles of leadership; those who expect participation and are motivated largely from within react best to participative or democratic leadership styles. Clearly, subordinates like nurses and technologists or other highly trained and professionalized health workers generally belong in the latter category.

THE CONGRUENCE OF OBJECTIVES.   When the objectives of the organization and those of its members are congruent, participative leadership practiced in a less formal structure is appropriate; but when organizational objectives and members' objectives are divergent, greater reliance must be placed upon authoritative leadership and a more formal organization structure. In highly professionalized organizations such as those providing health services there is much more congruence of objectives than in a manufacturing enterprise or a bank, for example. This means that, once again, the less formal participative style of leadership will usually be best.

These three considerations emphasize that there is no single successful style of leadership. Many factors contribute to its effectiveness. Personalities and expectations are important as are the situational or environmental factors. Of greatest importance, however, is the *attitude* of the leader himself, for he brings to his position a definite concept of the role of the leader. If his leadership style is going to be effective, he must be able to assess accurately the potentials of the situation and the capabilities and needs of his subordinates and choose his style accordingly.

Cultivating Leadership Attitudes

Since it is clear that attitudes of the leader are very important to successful leadership, the interpersonal relationships between leader and followers can be improved if the leader cultivates certain attitudes. Successful leaders realize that they get their job done through people and therefore try to develop social understanding and skills. They develop a healthy respect for people, if for no other reason than that their success as leaders depends on the cooperation of people. They approach problems in terms of the people involved even more than in terms of the technical aspects involved. There are two especially important attitudinal areas that the manager should try to cultivate: empathy and objectivity.

Empathy, in this context, means the ability to place one's self in the position of another, simulating that person's feelings, prejudices, and values. The manager without empathy for his subordinates assumes that his subordinates have the same objectives, ambitions, values, and so on that he has. Almost invariably this assumption is wrong. As the manager contemplates his subordinates in an attempt to understand their feelings and attitudes, he is severely handicapped. Outside of their work, the manager knows very little about his subordinates—their personal relationships, economic and health conditions, ambitions, loyalties, and so on. Placing one's self in the position of subordinates is indeed difficult. Yet a real and conscientious effort to understand a subordinate is much better than no effort at all. The simple act of the manager asking himself how he would react if he were the subordinate is an attempt to learn; with practice it will become a valuable skill.

Objectivity is an equally important attitude for the manager. He should try to observe and evaluate the causes of events unemotionally. This is difficult because the manager must depend heavily on subordinates, which often leads him to become emotional about them. It is very important, however, to evaluate from a distance, to be able to determine the real causes of events, and then to take intelligent steps to correct or to encourage as the case may be.

Obviously, the manager must walk a tightrope between empathy and objectivity. Empathy requires an attitude opposite to the remoteness and unemotional analysis necessary for objectivity. A workable balance between empathy and objectivity is difficult to achieve, but such a balance is essential to effective leadership.

COMMUNICATIONS ASPECTS OF THE
DIRECTING FUNCTION

We have seen that the exercise of leadership in the directing function *and* a thorough understanding of the way human motivation is intertwined with directing are both important. Yet no amount of expertise in these areas will suffice unless the manager is effective at communicating. In a very real sense, communicating is the key to directing. Unless what is to be done, how it is to be done, by whom it is to be done, and why it is to be done can all be effectively communicated, the chances of adequately carrying out the directing function are greatly reduced. Communicating depends upon formally establishing channels up and down the organization and then seeing that they work. This is a very complex and very important task.

Communication in highly complex health services organizations is a multidirectional process requiring movement downward, upward, and in all directions. It is a process of people relating to each other. As people relate to each other in doing work and in solving problems, they communicate facts, ideas, feelings, and attitudes. If this communication is adequate, the work gets done more effectively, and the problems are solved more efficiently. In an organized effort of any kind, communication is essential for people to work together because it permits them to influence each other and to react to each other.

Communication is vital to the directing function of management. But because of the relationship of directing to the other management functions, communication is important to them as well. One way to visualize this importance is to view the manager on one side of a barrier and the work group on the other. Communication is the means the manager has of reaching through the barrier to attain work group productivity. Figure 7-6 illustrates this.

Figure 7-6. Relationship of communication to management.

If the manager can communicate, then his efforts to perform the functions of management can be successful. If he cannot penetrate the barrier between manager and work group, then the functions cannot be effectively performed.

For a function so vital to managerial success, communication receives all too little attention by managers. As part of a larger study conducted by the author, the communication between superiors and subordinates in 17 large general hospitals was measured. The measurement was based on the degree of agreement on five basic aspects of the subordinate's function. The assumption was that if there was successful communication about these factors then there should be a high level of agreement about them. Table 7-1 contains the results of this study. As can be seen, there is poor agreement on such things as future changes in the subordinate's job and the obstacles in the way of the subordinate's performance of his job. This is empirical evidence of the extent of communication problems that exist in hospitals. It is reasonable to assume that similar results would be found in other types of health services organizations.

TABLE 7-1. *Percentage Distributions of Ratings Assigned to Superior-Subordinate Pairs on Five Basic Areas of the Subordinate's Job*

	0 Almost no agreement on topics	*1* Agreement on less than half the topics	*2* Agreement on about half the topics	*3* Agreement on more than half the topics	*4* Agreement on all or almost all the topics
Methods of Upward Communication	12.5	0	6.3	12.5	68.7
Job Duties	0	0	0	31.3	68.7
Job Requirements (Subordinate's Qualifications)	6.3	0	6.3	31.3	56.1
Future Changes in Subordinate's Job	75.0	0	18.7	0	6.3
Obstacles in Way of Subordinate's Performance	43.7	18.7	12.5	12.5	12.5

Communication Defined

By definition, *communication is the passing of information and understanding from a sender to a receiver.* Clearly, this definition does not restrict the concept to words alone, either written or spoken. It includes all methods by which meaning is conveyed from one person to another. Even silence can convey meaning and must be considered part of communicating.

A key point in this definition is that conveyed by the term "understanding." A sender will want his receiver to understand what was sent, which means that he wants the receiver to interpret the message exactly as the sender intended. Unfortunately, communication seldom results in complete understanding. This is true because there are so many factors that can prevent it. Many of these will be discussed as we continue. It is important for the manager to realize that he can make others hear him but he cannot *make* them understand him.

The communication process can be diagrammed easily, as seen in Figure 7-7. When communication is two-way (i.e., when there is an effective feedback), the chances that understanding will be transmitted are greatly enhanced. This is true because there is opportunity for the receiver to ask questions, seek additional information, and generally assure himself that he understands the message. It also provides the sender a means of judging whether his message has been received and understood or not.

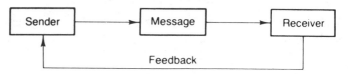

Figure 7-7. The communication process.

A number of barriers to communication exist in health services organizations. These barriers to communication can be broken down into (1) physical barriers and (2) psychological barriers. The physical barriers are those things that minimize the opportunities for communication to occur. These include, among other things, poor means of communication and time constraints that prevent the opportunity to communicate. They are relatively easy to remove once it is known that they exist.

A more difficult set of barriers are the psychological barriers. These usually arise from perceptual differences of persons in communicating relationships. Many of the problems are the result of attitudes and beliefs held by the sender or receiver. For example, the sender determines what he will communicate and how it will be phrased according to his perceptions of himself (his self-image), the image of the receiver, his concept of his own role in the organization, and the expected feedback and reactions to his communication.

Figure 7-8 points out some of the psychological barriers that exist in a situation where communication is taking place. Obviously, severe distortions of the message are possible as a result of psychological barriers.

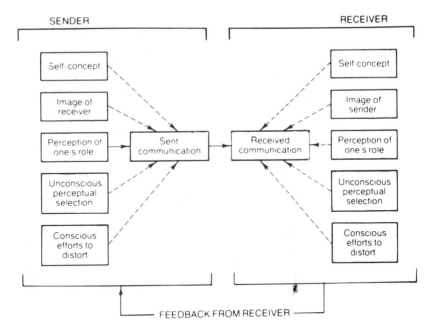

Figure 7-8. Psychological barriers to effective communication.

The Importance of Two-Way Communication

When a sender sends a message to a receiver who listens and then sends meaningful feedback to the sender, who also listens carefully, then there is effective two-way communication. This is important for the manager because good two-way communication is an absolute necessity for good human relations. Furthermore, it greatly enhances the likelihood that directives from the manager will be completely understood. There have been a number of studies that have demonstrated that the accuracy of work and, almost as importantly, the confidence in the accuracy of their work by employees are improved where effective two-way communication is practiced between managers and workers.

Oral vs. Written Communication

Communication flows in any direction via oral or written mechanisms. There are advantages and disadvantages to both. The directness of oral communications is unsurpassed. It is often face-to-face, which gives the communicants a chance to appraise the degree of understanding achieved, to ask questions, and to clarify meanings. Of course, oral communication is limited to those situations where time and the nature of the message permit direct contact. A further disadvantage is that perception of the spoken word is usually less accurate than perception of the written word.

There are some communications that must be made relatively permanent. These include reports, research information, policies, rules, and agreements. Written communications usually have the advantage of being more carefully thought through than oral communications, and the message can be checked for accuracy before it is sent. With written communications,, the sender and receiver do not have to have time to communicate simultaneously. This is important in a busy health services organization. On the other hand, there is the problem of keeping written communications up to date and the impossibility of always clarifying and elaborating meaning at the time the message is sent. There is also the problem of making certain that the receiver has read the written message.

One of the keys to good communication is the ability of the manager to exercise judgment in seeking a relative balance between the use of written and oral communications. His selection should be based on the relative success of the two methods in a given situation.

A great deal of written communication is in the form of reports that contain historical, current, or forecast information. Figure 7-9 illustrates the important role of written reports in health services organizations.

Informal Communication

Coexisting with the communication flows of formal organization is an informal communication flow commonly known as the grape vine. This term, by the way, arose during the Civil War when telegraph lines were strung between trees much like a grapevine. The messages transmitted over these flimsy lines were often garbled. As a result, any rumor was said to come from the "grapevine."[9]

The informal communication flows in an organization are as natural as the patterns of social interaction that develop. Like the

---

[9] Keith Davis, *Human Relations at Work: The Dynamics of Organizational Behavior* (New York: McGraw-Hill Book Company, 1967), p. 222.

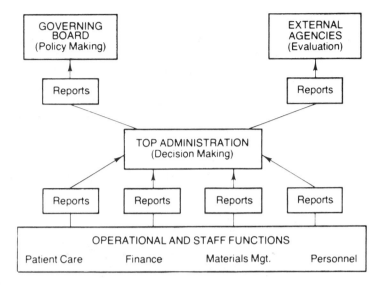

Figure 7-9. Functions of reports in the modern health services organization.

informal organization, the informal communication flows coexist with the formal patterns established by management.

The manager must realize that, good or bad, the grapevine is a fact of organizational life. "It cannot be abolished, rubbed out, hidden under a basket, chopped down, tied up, or stopped. If we suppress it in one place, it will pop up in another."[10]

Opinions about the grapevine vary. John Miner, for example, has said:

> There is very little that can be done to utilize the grapevine purposefully as a means of goal attainment. As a result, rumors probably do at least as much to subvert organizational goals as to foster them. They may well stir up dissension. They are contrary to fact.[11]

However, other authorities suggest that the informal communication flows are useful to the organization if properly managed. For downward flows, it tends to be much faster than the formal system; for upward and horizontal flows, it is essential. In health services organizations, much of the coordination that occurs between units in the organization comes about through the

---

[10] Keith Davis, *Human Behavior at Work*, 5th Edition, p. 278.

[11] John B. Miner, *Personnel Psychology* (New York: The Macmillan Company, 1969), p. 259.

informal give and take of information exchange. For upward flow, informal communication can be a rich source of information about the performance, ideas, feelings, and attitudes of people in the organization. Because of its potential usefulness, and because of its pervasive existence, managers should try to understand the informal communication flow and use it to advantage.

Keith Davis, who is one of the foremost authorities on informal communication, has suggested:

> Managers occasionally get the impression that the grapevine operates like a long chain in which A tells B, who tells C, who then tells D, and so on, until twenty persons later, Y gets the information—very late and very incorrect. Sometimes the grapevine may operate this way, but research shows that it generally follows a different pattern, which works something like this: A tells three or four others (such as B, R, and F) (as shown in Figure 7-10). Only one or two of these receivers will then pass on the information, and they will usually tell more than one person. Then as the information becomes older and the proportion of those knowing it gets larger, it gradually dies out because those who receive it do not repeat it. This network is a "cluster chain," because each link in the chain tends to inform a cluster of other people instead of only one person.[12]

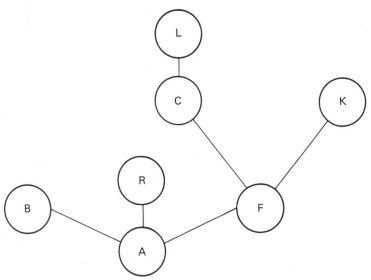

Figure 7-10. Cluster chain, the normal grapevine pattern.

From *Human Relations at Work: The Dynamics of Organizational Behavior* by Keith Davis. Copyright © 1967, McGraw-Hill Book Company. Used with permission of McGraw-Hill Book Company.

---

[12] Davis, *Human Relations*, p. 224.

In essence, the informal communication flow is present in every organization, it has good and bad potential for organizational effectiveness, and part of the manager's job is to use it to his advantage in achieving organization objectives.

Suggestions for Improving Organizational Communications

The following are ten suggestions that can help any manager improve his or her communication skills:

1. *Seek to clarify your ideas before communicating.* The more systematically we analyze the problem or idea to be communicated, the clearer it becomes. This is the first step toward effective communication. Many communications fail because of inadequate planning. Good planning must consider the goals and attitudes of those who will receive the communications and those who will be affected by it.

2. *Examine the true purpose of each communication.* Before you communicate, ask yourself what you really want to accomplish with your message—obtain information, initiate action, change another person's attitude? Identify your most important goal and then adapt your language, tone, and total approach to serve that specific objective. Don't try to accomplish too much with each communication. The sharper the focus of your message, the greater its chances of success.

3. *Consider the total physical and human setting whenever you communicate.* Meaning and intent are conveyed by more than words alone. Many other factors influence the overall impact of a communication, and the manager must be sensitive to the total setting in which he communicates. Consider, for example, your sense of timing—i.e., the circumstances under which you make an announcement or render a decision; the physical setting— whether you communicate in private, for example, or otherwise; the social climate that pervades work relationships within the [organization] or a department and sets the tone of its communications; custom and past practice—the degree to which your communication conforms to, or departs from, the expectations of your audience. Be constantly aware of the total setting in which you communicate. Like all living things, communication must be capable of adapting to its environment.

4. *Consult with others, where appropriate, in planning communications.* Frequently it is desirable or necessary to seek the participation of others in planning a communication or developing the facts on which to base it. Such consultation often helps to lend additional insight and objectivity to your message. Moreover, those who have helped you plan your communication will give it their support.

5. *Be mindful, while you communicate, of the overtones as well as the basic content of your message.* Your tone of voice, your expression, your apparent receptivenesss to the responses of others—all have tremendous impact on those you wish to reach. Frequently overlooked, these subtleties of communication often affect a listener's reaction to a message even more than its basic content. Similarly, your choice of language—particularly your awareness of the fine shades of meaning and emotion in the words you use—predetermines in large part the reactions of your listeners.

6. *Take the opportunity, when it arises, to convey something of help or value to the receiver.* Consideration of the other person's interests and needs—the habit of trying to look at things from his point of view—will frequently point up opportunities to convey something of immediate benefit or long-range value to him. People on the job are most responsive to the manager whose messages take their own interests into account.

7. *Follow up your communication.* Our best efforts at communication may be wasted, and we may never know whether we have succeeded in expressing our true meaning and intent, if we do not follow up to see how well we have put our message across. This you can do by asking questions, by encouraging the receiver to express his reactions, by follow-up contacts, by subsequent review of performance. Make certain that every important communication has a feedback so that complete understanding and appropriate action result.

8. *Communicate for tomorrow as well as today.* While communications may be aimed primarily at meeting the demands of an immediate situation, they must be planned with the past in mind if they are to maintain consistency in the receiver's view; but, most important of all, they must be consistent with long-range interests and goals. For example, it is not easy to communicate frankly on such matters as poor performance or the shortcomings of a loyal subordinate—but postponing disagreeable communications makes them more difficult in the long run and is actually unfair to your subordinates and your [health services organization].

9. *Be sure your actions support your communications.* In the final analysis, the most persuasive kind of communication is not what you say but what you do. When a man's actions or attitudes contradict his words, we tend to discount what he has said. For every manager this means that good supervisory practices—such as clear assignment of responsibility—authority, fair rewards for effort, and sound policy enforcement—serve to communicate more than all the gifts of oratory.

10. *Last, but by no means least: Seek not only to be understood but to understand—be a good listener.* When we start talking we often cease to listen—in that larger sense of being attuned to the other person's unspoken reactions and attitudes. Even more serious is the fact that we are all guilty, at times, of inattentiveness when others are attempting to communicate to us. Listening is one of the most important, most difficult—and most

neglected—skills in communication. It demands that we concentrate not only on the explicit meanings another person is
expressing, but on the implicit meanings, unspoken words, and
undertones that may be far more significant. Thus we must learn
to listen with the inner ear if we are to know the inner man.[13]

SUMMARY

Directing is the management function that initiates action in the
organization. Specifically, it means the issuance of orders, asign-
ments, and instructions that permit the subordinate to understand
what is expected of him and the guidance and overseeing of the
subordinate so that he can contribute effectively and efficiently to
the attainment of the objectives of the health services organization.

Since the management function of directing is the interpersonal aspect of managing, it is quite complex. Success at directing
will be largely determined by the manager's understanding of
human nature and by his attitude toward subordinates. Issuing
orders and delegation are the two techniques the manager has at
his disposal in directing his subordinates.

We have seen that leadership is the accomplishment of organizational objectives through interpersonal relationships between
the leader and those he leads. A leader's personal traits help
determine the quality of leadership, but so do those of the followers, their objectives, and the situation in which leadership is
practiced. Leadership styles can take many forms along a continuum ranging from the completely authoritarian style with no
subordinate participation to the maximum degree of democratic
leadership that enables the subordinate to participate in all phases
of the decision-making process. The appropriate leadership style is
largely determined by the organizational environment, the personalities of those involved, and the congruence of the objectives of
the organization and those who work in it. Finally, it is important
that the leader cultivate attitudes which permit him or her to
balance empathy with objectivity as he or she leads subordinates.

Effective communication is essential to the directing function
of management. It is the passing of information and understanding from a sender to a receiver. The process itself is simple, but the
physical and psychological barriers to good communication often
make it a demanding management activity.

---

[13] "Ten Commandments of Good Communication," (New York: American Management Association, 1955).

The manager must be aware of the advantages and disadvantages of written and oral communications in various situations and select the appropriate method. The manager's communications are usually enhanced by a two-way flow of information between the sender and receiver.

There are a number of steps which can be taken to improve communications. Among the most important are:

1. Clarify in your own mind what you want to communicate. This includes being certain of what you want the communication to accomplish.

2. Use all reasonable means to convey not only information but understanding.

3. Follow up your communications and be certain that your actions support your communications.

4. Remember that often it is equally, if not more, important to be a good listener than speaker. Feedback is crucial to good communication.

Coordinating: The Essence of Management

EIGHT

The Head Nurses filed into the conference room for their weekly meeting with the Director of Nursing. After giving status reports on several issues that confronted the Nursing Service, the Director turned her attention to a topic that had not been on the agenda—coordination.

"I want to tell you about an incident that occurred yesterday afternoon," she said. "Luther Fillerey's surgeon stopped me as I was leaving for a meeting to complain about the fact that she was not called by the night shift nurses the night Mr. Fillerey died. We've got to do a better job of coordinating between shifts than that."

The Head Nurse for Fillerey's unit said, "I don't remember passing the word about that along. Of course, we have to get so much information to the other shifts that I could have forgotten. Anyway, our usual policy is to call the Chief Resident and that's what the night shift nurse did—we get so busy sometimes that not everything can be perfectly coordinated."

The Director quickly added, "I'm not trying to place the blame on anybody. I'm simply using this to illustrate how important it is for us to coordinate things between the shifts."

Another Head Nurse raised the point, "Coordination between us and the other departments seems to be a more serious problem than coordination between shifts of nurses. Last week we had a patient who had to be rescheduled for a barium enema because somebody forgot to tell food service that he wasn't suppose to get lunch until after the radiology people were through with him."

The Head Nurse on the Pediatric Unit also voiced her concern, "The lab people always come around to draw blood just at the time we start morning baths for our patients. It's hectic enough at that time without having them around drawing blood."

The Director responded, "I've talked to the Laboratory Director about that problem before. He always tells me that if they don't draw the blood early in the morning, then they can't get the tests done in time for the afternoon rounds by the doctors. It's a problem we'll just have to live with."

The meeting continued for almost an hour with every Head Nurse revealing at least one coordination problem on her unit. The meeting adjourned at 10:30 a.m. with the Director agreeing to bring up the topic of coordination at the next Department Head's Meeting.

INTRODUCTION

In the typical health services organization—which is made up of diverse participants and activities—a central management function is that of coordinating the various participants and activities so that they are all channeled in mutually supportive directions. Coordination is the management function of synchronizing differentiated activities and diverse participants so that they function smoothly in the attainment of the organization's objectives.

As Fayol described it years ago, the act of coordinating pulls together all the activities of the enterprise to make possible both its working and its success.[1] Ordway Tead says that coordination is "the effort to assure a smooth interplay of the functions and forces of all the different component parts of an organization to the end that its purposes will be realized with a minimum of friction and a maximum of collaborative effectiveness."[2] Coordination pertains to the synchronization of the actions of people within an organization, and one of the important goals of every management is to achieve this synchronization or coordination. Charns and Schaefer note that "in health care organizations, coordination among different groups of providers and between providers and support services encompass critical interconnections in the delivery of care. How well these are addressed contributes directly to organizational performance."[3]

Coordination is not easily attained. Each special departmental interest in an organization stresses its own opinion of how the organization's purposes should be accomplished, and each tends

---

[1] Henri Fayol, *General and Industrial Management,* trans. Constance Storrs (London: Sir Isaac Pitman and Sons, Ltd., 1949), p. 104.

[2] Ordway Tead, *Administration: Its Purpose and Performance* (New York: Harper and Brothers, 1959), p. 36.

[3] Martin P. Charns and Marguerite J. Schaefer, *Health Care Organizations: A Model for Management* (Englewood Cliffs, NJ: Prentice-Hall, Inc., 1983), p. 144.

to favor one policy or another depending upon its function and viewpoint. Haimann and Scott say:

> The problem of the different viewpoints applies both in and among the several levels in a managerial hierarchy. It takes real thoughtfulness, listening power, and good will to see and understand a problem of work relationships with the group above or below. In spite of cooperative attitudes and self-coordination or self-adjustment by each member of a group, there will be duplication of action and conflicts of efforts unless management synchronizes all of them. Through coordination, management can bring about a total accomplishment far in excess of the sum of the individual parts. Each part has significance, but the result can be of much greater significance if management achieves success at coordination.[4]

TYPES OF COORDINATION

It is important to note that coordinative activity varies within and among organizations according to the objectives toward which it is directed and the motivations that underlie it. For example, one can initiate coordinative activity in response to an existing problem or to prevent an anticipated problem. It may be initiated without any reference to a particular problem. Therefore, it is possible to group coordinative activities into various types. Georgopoulos and Mann have developed a classification of four types of coordination. They are: corrective, preventive, regulatory, and promotive coordination.[5]

Corrective coordination is defined as those coordinative activities that rectify an error or correct a dysfunction in the organization after it has occurred. In contrast, preventive coordination is defined as those coordinative activities that are aimed at preventing the occurrence of anticipated problems of coordination or, at least, minimizing the impact of these problems. Regulatory coordination is defined as those coordinative activities that are aimed at the maintenance of existing structural and functional arrangements in the organization. It does not require cognizance of any particular malfunctions or problems, whether in retrospect or anticipation. The fourth type of coordination, promotive coordination, is defined as those coordinative activities that attempt to improve the articulation of the parts of the organization, or to improve the existing organizational arrangements without regard

---

[4] Theo Haimann and William G. Scott, *Management in the Modern Organization* (Boston: Houghton Mifflin Company, 1970), p. 167.

[5] Basil S. Georgopoulos and Floyd C. Mann, *The Community General Hospital* (New York: The Macmillan Company, 1962), pp. 277-278.

for specific problems. Such coordinative activity does not stem from an awareness of particular problems in the organization. Rather, it stems from the simple assumption that the organization is imperfectly coordinated at any given time and that there is always room for improvement.

In a research study conducted by the author, the relationships of these four types of coordination to efficiency and quality were investigated. It was found that those organizations that use preventive and promotive coordination provide higher quality of care and provide it more efficiently than those which rely more on corrective coordination.[6]

CONFLICT IN HEALTH SERVICES ORGANIZATIONS

When coordination fails, or is ineffective, conflict results. Conflict may be defined, in broad terms, as all kinds of opposition or antagonistic interaction. Most health services organizations, because of the tremendously complex organizational structure and the diversity of participants, experience a rather high level of conflict. Schultz and Johnson, writing about hospitals, for example, have stated:

> Evidence of conflict in hospitals is readily apparent. Nurse and nonprofessional hospital employee strikes receive wide publicity. Periodically, administrator-medical staff conflicts break into public view. Furthermore, hospital-client conflicts seem to be increasing as consumers of hospital services level charges of inefficiency and inattention to consumer expectations.[7]

The same can be said about most modern health services organizations.

Attitudes about the role of conflict in organizations are diverse and are undergoing a transition with the passage of time. The early management theorists had a straightforward attitude. During the period prior to the mid-1940's, almost all management thinkers (with the notable exception of Mary Parker Follett) saw all conflict as destructive and viewed management's role as one of ridding the organization of conflict.

---

[6] Beaufort B. Longest, Jr., "Relationships Between Coordination, Efficiency, and Quality of Care in General Hospitals," *Hospital Administration,* Fall 1974, pp. 65-86.

[7] Rockwell Schultz and Alton C. Johnson, "Conflict in Hospitals," *Hospital Administration,* Summer 1971, p. 36.

The traditional approach was followed by the behavioral view, which is still the most prevalent view about managing conflict in modern organizations. Essentially, this approach reflects an acceptance of conflict as a fact of organizational life. It is unquestionably a fact in the complex health services organization. Disagreements over objectives for the organization can be found among administrators, trustees, physicians, nurses, and other participants. Departments and individuals compete for recognition, prestige, and power. Empires are built, often at the expense of some other part of the organization.

The behaviorists seek to rationalize conflict. For example, Katz has said, " . . . it should be added that we are not assuming that all conflict is bad and that the only objective toward which we should work is the resolution of conflict. Group conflict has positive social functions . . . "[8]

The newest approach to conflict, one which is not taken by very many managers, is a more positive approach called the "interactionist philosophy" by Stephen P. Robbins. He suggests that the interactionist philosophy differs from the behavioral viewpoint in that it:[9]

1. Recognizes the absolute necessity of conflict,
2. Explicitly encourages opposition,
3. Defines conflict management to include stimulation as well as resolution methods, and
4. Considers the management of conflict as a major responsibility of all managers.

The interactionists accept and sometimes encourage conflict by recognizing that just as the level of conflict may be too high and require reduction, it may also be too low and in need of increased intensity. The interactionists believe organizations that do not stimulate conflict increase the probability of stagnant thinking, inadequate decisions and, in extreme cases, organizational demise.

The problem with conflict in hospitals and other types of health care organizations is that it can affect the quality of patient care. Georgopoulos and Mann, for instance, have found higher quality in hospitals where physicians and nurses have a greater understanding of each other's work, problems, and needs.[10] Stud-

---

[8] Chapter 9, "Approaches to Managing Conflict," by Daniel Katz in *Power and Conflict in Organizations,* edited by Robert L. Kahn, and Elise Boulding, (New York: Foundation on Human Behavior, Basic Books, Inc., 1964).

[9] Stephen P. Robbins, *Managing Organizational Conflict* (Englewood Cliffs, NJ: Prentice-Hall, Inc., 1974), p. 13.

[10] Georgopoulos and Mann, *The Community General Hospital,* p. 400.

ies in mental hospitals report that patients are affected adversely by staff conflict.[11] The task for the manager is to balance the level of conflict so that the positive benefits (chiefly innovative organizational change as described in Chapter 10) can be achieved without disrupting the quality of patient care. As one might expect, this is an extremely difficult task.

ACHIEVING ORGANIZATIONAL COORDINATION

Organizations typically establish several different mechanisms for achieving coordination. Litterer suggests three primary means: through the hierarchy, the administrative system, and voluntary activities.[12] In hierarchical coodination, the various activities are linked together by placing them under a central authority. In a simple organization, this form of coordination might be sufficient. However, in the complex organizations, such as most health services organizations, with many levels and numerous specialized departments, hierarchical coordination becomes more difficult. Although the administrator is a focal point of authority, at least for the administrative hierarchy of the facility, it would be impossible for him to cope with all the coordinating problems that might come up through the hierarchy. Thus, coordination through the hierarchical structure must be supplemented by other means.

The administrative system provides a second mechanism for coordination of activities. Much of the effort expended by managers to coordinate is made through formal procedures ("administrative systems" in Litterer's words) which achieve coordination almost automatically. Many work procedures such as memoranda with routing slips help coordinate efforts to different operating units. To the extent that these procedures can be programmed or routinized, it is not necessary to establish specific means for coordination.

A third type of coordination is through voluntary means. Sometimes, an individual or group of individuals sees a problem, finds a solution, and applies it. Much of the coordination may depend upon the willingness and ability of individuals or groups to voluntarily find means of integrating their activities with those of other organizational participants. Achieving voluntary coordination is one of the most important yet difficult problems of the manager. Voluntary coordination requires that the individual have sufficient

[11] Alfred H. Stanton and Morris S. Schwartz, *The Mental Hospital* (New York: Basic Books, Inc., 1954), pp. 342-365.
[12] Joseph A. Litterer, *The Analysis of Organizations* (New York: John Wiley and Sons, 1965), pp. 223-232.

knowledge of organizational goals and objectives, adequate information concerning the specific problems of coordination, and the motivation to do something on his own. The high degree of professionalism among many health organization participants accounts to a large extent for the voluntary coordination that takes place in an organization whose structure would seem, in many instances, to make coordination impossible.

Another approach to coordinating activities is the committee. Committees typically are made up of members from a number of different departments or functional areas and are concerned with problems requiring coordination. The use of committees for purposes of coordination is a well-established approach in health care institutions. It is so important, in fact, that we will have a special section on it later in this chapter.

Additional means for coordination have developed in many organizations. Lawrence and Lorsch[13] have studied six organizations operating in the chemical processing industry to determine how they achieve coordination. These organizations use a technology that requires activities that are highly differentiated and specialized but which also have a major degree of integration among them. (They are similar to most health services organizations in this way.) The study was concerned with how organizations achieve both substantial differentiation and tight coordination when these forces seem paradoxical. They found that successful companies use task forces, teams, and project offices to achieve coordination. There is a tendency to formalize coordinative activities that have developed informally and voluntarily. In the most successful organizations, the influence of the integrators (those people who seem to hold the key to successful coordination) stems from their professional competence rather than from their formal position. They are successful as integrators because of their specialized knowledge and because they represent a central source of information in the operation. These results suggest that it is possible for complex organizations such as health care facilities to achieve both differentiation of activities and effective coordination; however, new organizational arrangements which make greater use of specialized knowledge, like that of health professionals, might be required in order to do so.

Others have recommended new structural forms to help with the problems of coordination. Likert feels that one mechanism for achieving coordination is having people serve as "linking pins"

---

[13] Paul R. Lawrence and J. W. Lorsch, "Differentiation and Integration in Complex Organizations," *Administrative Science Quarterly,* June 1967, pp. 1-47.

between the various units of the organization.[14] Horizontally, there are certain organizational participants who are members of two separate groups and serve as coordinating agents between them. On the vertical basis, individuals serve as linking pins between their own level and those above and below. Thus, through this system of linking pins, the voluntary coordination necessary to make the dynamic system operate effectively is achieved. This forms a multiple, overlapping group structure in the organization. Likert says:

> To perform the intended coordination well, a fundamental require-
> ment must be met. The entire organization must consist of a
> multiple, overlapping group structure with *every* work group using
> group decision-making processes skillfully. This requirement applies
> to the functional, product, and service departments. An organization
> meeting this requirement will have an effective interaction-influence
> system through which the relevant communications flow readily, the
> required influence is exerted laterally, upward, and downward, and
> the motivational forces needed for coordination are created.[15]

The Committee as a Means of Coordination

Health services organizations make considerable use of committees to achieve coordination. The governing board of the typical
health services organization, as well as the medical staff, is
organized on the basis of committees. In addition, the organization has many standing and *ad hoc* committees and the various
departments and sub-units of the organization rely heavily on
committees. Committees serve other purposes besides coordination; they may act in a service, advisory, infomational, or decision-
making capacity. However, their chief purpose is coordination. The
committee is a formally designated group; therefore, the reader
may wish to review the material in Chapter 6 on small groups. It
should be pointed out that although the material in Chapter 6
pertains directly to the formation of small *informal* groups, committees (which are formally designated groups) take on many of the
characteristics of small informal groups. Committees, and their
work, are aften criticized as being ineffective. For example, it has
been said that the best committee is a five-man committee with
four members absent. The classical theorist, Luther Gulick, wanted
to limit the use of committees to abnormal situations because he

---

[14] Rensis Likert, *The Human Organization* (New York: McGraw-Hill Book Company, 1967), p. 156.

[15] *Ibid.,* p. 167.

thought they were too dilatory, irresponsible, and time-consuming for normal administration.[16] Urwick was an even harsher critic. He listed no fewer than fourteen faults of committees, the main ones being that committees are often irresponsible, are apt to be bad employers, and are costly.[17] Thus the classicists tended to emphasize the negative, but the more modern view recognizes that committees have both positive and negative attributes.

Committees are time-consuming and expensive. The next time you are in a committee meeting, calculate the man-hours and the cost in salaries alone of the meeting (some of you may see this as an unnecessary, time-consuming and expensive exercise—but just this sort of thing does go on in meetings!).

From an organizational standpoint, there are some potential problems inherent in committees. The most obvious is divided responsibility. This is to say that often in a committee, there is group responsibility or accountability but not individual responsibility. Thus, critics argue, the committee in reality turns out to have no responsibility or accountability. In fact, individuals may use the committee as a shield to avoid personal responsibility for bad decisions or mistakes. One solution to this problem is to make all committee members responsible, and another is to hold the chairperson responsible. Both approaches have many obvious difficulties. For example, if the entire committee is held responsible for a wrong decision, what about the individual members who voted against the majority? Holding them accountable for the committee's decision could have disastrous effects on their morale, but holding only those who voted for a particular decision responsible would create an inhibiting effect that would destroy the value of committee action.

Besides being time-consuming, costly, and having divided responsibility, committees may reach decisions that are products of excessive compromise, logrolling, and one-man or minority domination. This represents the reverse of the advantages of integrated group judgment and pooling of specialized knowledge. Where unanimity is either formally required or an informal group norm, the difficulties are compounded. A final decision may be so extremely watered down or "compromised to death" that it is

---

[16] Luther Gulick, "Notes on the Theory of Organization," in Luther Gulick and L. Urwick (eds.), *Papers on the Science of Administration* (New York: Institute of Public Administration, 1937), p. 36.

[17] Lyndall F. Urwick, "Committees in Organization," reprinted from the *British Management Review* by Management Journals, Ltd., 1933, p. 14; and *The Elements of Administration* (New York: Harper & Row Publishers, Inc., 1943), pp. 71-72.

ineffective. The strength of committee action comes through a synthesis and integration of divergent viewpoints, not through a compromise of the least common denominator. One way to avoid the problem is to limit the committee to serving as a forum for the exchange of information and ideas. Another possibility is to let the chairman have the final decision-making prerogative. Yet these solutions are not always satisfactory because, when the committee is charged with making a decision, considerable social skill and a willingness to cooperate fully must exist if good, effective decisions are to evolve.

Given these problems with committees, why do health services organizations make such wide use of them? The obvious answer is that there are some benefits that outweigh the problems. In many cases, committee action has a number of advantages over individual action. One of its most important attributes is the combined and integrated judgment which committee action makes possible. Members can bring a wide range of experience, knowledge, ability, and personality characteristics to bear on problems which the committee is faced with solving. There is evidence that brainstorming (which a committee structure facilitates) yields more creative solutions to problems than individuals working alone.

From a human standpoint, the biggest advantage of committees may be the increased motivation and commitment derived from participation. By being involved in the analysis and solution of committee problems, individual members will more readily accept and try to implement what has been decided. A committee can also be instrumental in human development and growth. Group members, especially the young and inexperienced, can take advantage of observing and learning from other members with more experience or with different viewpoints and knowledge. A committee provides the opportunity for personal development that the individual would never receive on his own.

The most important attribute of committees in health services organizations is the promotion of coordination between departments and sub-units of the organization. In effect, committees foster communication. Through committee discussion, each member has an opportunity to better understand the purposes and problems faced by others in the organization and to see the interrelatedness of various participants and activities in the organization.

Committee functioning and the contribution of individuals to committee work can be enhanced by a better understanding of the way committees work. Research has shown that they are most effective when the chairperson exerts considerable influence and does not attempt to share this role with others.[18] A certain amount of "take-charge" attitude seems required, along with a focusing on task considerations. Generally, chairpeople perceived as fulfilling role expectations, structuring activities, and exercising control are viewed as more skillful.

An analysis of group dynamics literature indicates several other conditions for effective committee operation:

1. A clearly defined committee task should exist.
2. Members should be selected so as to have some definite relationship to task accomplishment.
3. Superiors and subordinates should not serve on the same committee, but the fact that a manager holds a position at a given level should not in and of itself be a basis for inclusion.
4. Committees must have time to evolve interpersonal relationships before they can move on effectively to problem solutions.
5. To function most effectively, committees require the support of those groups or individuals to whom the results of their deliberations are to be submitted.
6. Committees with a task to perform should be clearly differentiated from those whose major role is to develop the managerial competence of members.[19]

PROFESSIONALISM AND COORDINATION

The means of achieving coordination (and thereby controlling conflict) outlined above are useful techniques. However, given the degree of complexity of health services organizations, they are not enough. In order to deal with unusual and non-routine events, it is necessary to have a high level of voluntary coordination and a willingness to work effectively with others. Writing about hospitals (although their comments are equally applicable to all kinds of health care facilities), Georgopoulos and Mann have said, "The hospital is dependent very greatly upon the motivations and voluntary, informal adjustments of its members for the attainment and maintenance of good coordination. Formal organizational plans, rules, regulations, and controls may ensure some minimum coordination, but of themselves are incapable of producing adequate coordination, for only a fraction of all the coordinative activities required in this organization can be programmed in

---

[18] G.M. Prince, "How to be a Better Chairman," *Harvard Business Review,* January-February 1969), pp. 98-108.

[19] John B. Miner, *The Management Process: Theory, Research, and Practice* (New York: The Macmillan Company, 1978), p. 322.

advance."[20] One of the primary forces ensuring voluntary coordination is the overall value system supportive of the patient's welfare, which is developed through the training and professionalization of health professionals.

SUMMARY

In a complex health services organization, with a diversity of participants and activities, coordination is a critically important concern for the manager. We have defined coordination as the management function of synchronizing differentiated activities and diverse participants so that they function smoothly in the attainment of the organization's objectives. There are several basic approaches to coordination: corrective, preventive, regulatory, and promotive.

The end result of inadequate coordination is conflict, which is defined as all kinds of opposition or antagonistic interaction. The manager must realize that conflict can be harmful *but* that it also has some positive benefits to the organization. The chief benefit of conflict is the stimulation of innovative organizational change.

There are several mechanisms through which the organization can achieve coordinated effort. The most basic way is through the hierarchy of the organization (someone is given authority over a set of people and activities). In complex organizations this usually has to be supported by other mechanisms, such as through the administrative system, which automatically carries out a good deal of the necessary coordinative activity. Also, in health services organizations, the high degree of professionalism leads to a significant amount of voluntary coordination, especially where the patient care activity is involved. The committee is used in health services organizations to achieve coordination, among other things. The committee approach fosters communication among the participants and thus can improve coordination.

[20] Basil S. Georgopoulos and Floyd C. Mann, "The Hospital as an Organization," *Hospital Administration,* Fall 1962, pp. 57-58.

Controlling:
The Straight and Narrow Path

NINE

**JUNE 1ST
4:30 P.M.** The Medical Audit Committee Chairman, opening the meeting said, "Today the Administrator has asked us to review the Fillerey case and to develop recommendations on how to preclude such serious lapses in our quality control program." He then turned to the Administrator and asked for a status report on the case.

The Administrator stood up and said, "As you know, we have settled this case out of court. This was done on the advice of our insurance company and our attorney. The surgeon's insurance company has also settled with the Fillerey family so that both suits have been dropped. The thing for us to do now is to try to look at the situation, determine where our quality control system went wrong, and develop recommendations that would prevent such a thing from happening again."

One of the Physician members spoke at that point. "It concerns me that we are always looking at cases as past history. This one is no exception. It seems to me that good quality control would prevent such things as what happened to Luther Fillerey."

Another Physician agreed. "You're exactly right! I've reviewed this case, as everyone in this room has, and I think we all know what went wrong. Central Supply fouled up by not properly sterilizing the instrument; the Surgeon fouled up by failing to diagnose the infection that resulted; and the nurses fouled up by not keeping a close enough watch on Fillerey to see that he was going sour that night before it was too late for anybody to do anything about it!"

"You're saying," asked the Chairman, "that even if we find out what happened in this case and take steps to prevent it from happening again that it isn't enough to prevent other equally disastrous foul-ups?"

"Yes!"

"I agree with you," said the Chairman, "there is only so much that can be controlled."

"And control costs money," said the Administrator, "I guess the ideal situation would be to have one person do something and another check on him all along the way."

"That's not very practical!" rejoined one member.

"I know it isn't," retorted the Administrator, "I'm just saying that control is not very easy to pull off. We don't have the money, the people, or the time to do it in a comprehensive way."

At that point the Chairman said, "Let's cool down here and remember the job at hand."

The Committee reviewed every piece of written information they had on the Luther J. Fillerey case and discussed it at great length. By 6:30 p.m., they had agreed on the series of events that led to the death of Luther J. Fillerey, but as they adjourned, the only recommendation for the Administrator was that it would be very important to keep everyone on their toes about quality control.

INTRODUCTION

If the plans made to meet organizational objectives were always conceived and executed flawlessly by an ideally structured organization where perfect coordination was achieved under the direction of an omnipotent leader, there would be no need for control. So far, no organization has achieved this Utopian state. Until one does, all organizations will require the management function of controlling. In organizations involved with the delivery of health services, the control function takes on an even greater importance. This results from the ever present necessity to control the quality of care given so that the highest standards of care can be achieved and provided on a routine basis. Furthermore, as we discussed in Chapter 1, the limited resources available to meet the health care needs of our society make it absolutely necessary that close control be maintained over the costs of providing health services in the organizational setting. Quality of care and cost of care are not the only factors that managers must control. They are, however, the most important factors in organizations set up to deliver health services. Thus, they will be described at length in this chapter as examples of how the controlling function of the management process takes place. Before these two applications are described, we should develop some basic concepts of controlling as a management function.

Controlling can be defined as the regulation of activities in accordance with the requirements of plans. By definition, controlling is directly linked to the planning function. This can be seen diagrammatically in Figure 9-1.

The managerial function of control consists of measuring and correcting the activities of people and things in the organization to make certain that objectives and the plans made to attain them are accomplished. It is a function of all managers on all levels, and its basic purpose is to ensure that what is intended to be done is what is done. The word "control" often carries a negative connotation. People frequently think of it as a somewhat sinister activity involv-

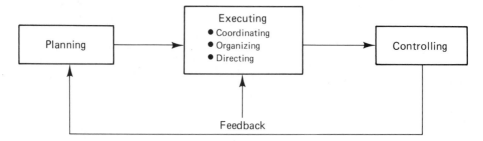

Figure 9—1. The relationship of controlling to planning.

ing surveillance, correction, or even reproach. In truth, it need not be viewed in this way at all. Newman has described the real nature of control as a management function in the following way:

1. *Control is a normal, pervasive, and positive force.* Evaluation of results accomplished and feedback of this information to those who can influence future results is a natural phenomenon. The cook watches the pie in the oven, the orchestra conductor listens to his orchestra—and its recordings; the doctor checks his patient; the oil refiner tests the quality of his end-product; the farmer counts his chickens; the football coach keeps an eye on the scoreboard...

2. *Managerial control is effective only when it guides someone's behavior.* Behavior, not measurements and reports, is the essence of control. We often become so involved with the mechanics of control that we lose sight of its purpose. Unless one or more persons act differently than they otherwise would, the control reports have no impact. Consequently, when we think about designing and implementing control, we must always ask ourselves, "Who is going to behave differently, and what will be the nature of his response?"....

3. *Successful control is future-oriented and dynamic.* Long before the Apollo spacecraft reached the moon, control adjustments had been made.... We use early measurements to predict where our present course is leading, and modify inputs to keep us on target....

4. *Control relates to all sorts of human endeavors.* The need for evaluation and feedback is just as pressing in charitable organizations as in profit-seeking corporations. Each is concerned with attaining its goals and each has limited resources. Moreover, control should not be confined to easy-to-measure results. The quality of service in a hospital or bank, the training and promotion of minority workers, and the resourcefulness of a purchasing agent in developing alternative sources for important supplies— all need to be controlled.[1]

---

[1] William H. Newman, *Constructive Control: Design and Use of Control Systems* (Englewood Cliffs, NJ: Prentice-Hall, Inc., 1975), pp. 3-5. Reprinted by permission of Prentice-Hall, Inc., Englewood Cliffs, New Jersey.

STEPS IN THE CONTROL FUNCTION

The control function, whether it is applied to cash, medical care, employee morale, or anything else, involves four steps: (1) establishing standards, (2) measuring performance, (3) comparing actual results with standards, and (4) correcting deviations from standards. Figure 9-2 illustrates these steps.

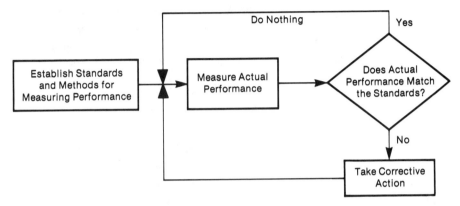

Figure 9–2. Basic steps in control function.

Standards can be defined as established criteria against which actual results can be compared. They are, in essence, the expression of objectives in terms that actual performance can be measured against. Such standards can be quantity, cost, time, or quality measures. They are usually expressed in specific units, but this need not always be the case. For example, a manager may have the objective of a high level of employee morale. Standards can be set for such objectives although probably not in numerical terms. Furthermore, means of determining whether action is toward or away from such objectives can be devised. These kinds of standards are much more difficult to quantify and measure than some others, but the managerial benefits make it worth the effort.

If standards are realistically developed and if means are available for determining exactly what subordinates are doing, measuring performance and comparing actual results with standards is fairly easy. In many situations, however, the nature of the activity is such that establishing standards and measuring performance are difficult.

Ideally, comparison will discover no significant deviations. If they are found, then corrective action must be taken. The purpose of such action is to either correct deviations from planned performance or alter the plan to allow for obstacles which cannot be removed. The point at which corrective action is taken is where control blends with the other management functions. The manager may correct by altering his plans or modifying the objective from which the plan derived. He may correct through the organizing function—through reassignment of duties, additional staffing, or better training of employees. He may correct through more careful coordination. Finally, he may correct through better direction such as a more complete explanation of the job or more effective leadership. This overlap of the control function with the other management functions illustrates the unity of the manager's job. Having taken a broad overview of the controlling function, perhaps we should look at each of its four steps in some detail.

ESTABLISHING STANDARDS

Standards are criteria against which to judge results. In carrying out the planning function, management sets the objectives that it hopes to meet. The most important idea in control is to determine to some extent what should result, or at least what is expected from a given action.

There are a great many different types of standards. Sometimes they may be general qualitative standards in areas such as attitudes, morale, or interdepartmental relationships. These types of standards have the obvious problem of a lack of precision, which make them difficult to establish and utilize. Nevertheless, management must not overlook the importance of intangible standards in achieving a balanced control over their responsibilities.

In many situations it is possible to set standards that are quantitative. This means that they can be stated in specific units, such as a certain number of procedures per hour or a certain cost per procedure. Obviously, if enough thought is given, standards can be developed for virtually any activity, and, whether they are quantitative or qualitative, they can be useful in the control function.

There is such a large variety of possible standards that it is necessary for the manager to be selective. It is literally impossible to check the performance of each activity against all of the possible standards which might be applied to it. The technical term for those chosen for control purposes is "strategic control standards." This means simply that the manager should select those standards that best reflect the objectives he is trying to meet and that best show whether or not they are being met. The standards selected should be timely, economical, and permit comprehensive and balanced control.

Timeliness is necessary so that adjustments can be made before serious damage is done. Another important reason for timeliness is that controlling should be a learning experience. When deviations are quickly detected, corrective action can be prompt. Everyone can learn from the experience, which would not be as likely if controlling occurred at a later time when the situation was not still familiar to the participants.

In view of the limited resources with which most managers are faced, economy is important in selecting standards as it is in performing all management functions. One of the reasons for controlling is to keep costs at an acceptable level; therefore it makes no sense to overspend on controlling.

Finally, it is necessary to select a range of strategic standards that will permit comprehensive and balanced control. The manager can be guided in part by his or her experience and knowledge of jobs to be performed within his or her department. Most managers have a general idea as to how much time it takes to perform certain jobs, how much material is required, and what constitutes good quality of performance. Thus, job knowledge and experience are major sources for establishing the standards by which a manager judges performance within his department. He might also use previous budgets and departmental records to help him arrive at standards of performance.

There are other more scientific and systematic ways of establishing standards. Job analysis is the process of gathering information on all aspects of a specific job. One of the purposes of job analysis and measurement is to set standards for specific jobs. They represent the amount and quality of work expected of an employee. Essentially, standards aid in planning the work of a department and determining the number of employees needed. Only work that meets the following criteria should be measured and standardized:

1. The work is repetitive.

2. The content is uniform and consistent.

3. The work can be measured (i.e., it is discernible in quantitative terms).

4. Finally, the volume of work must be large enough to warrant the expense of measuring and standardizing.

Measuring Work and Setting Standards

There are a number of methods of measuring work and setting standards. Among them are: (1) analysis of past production records, (2) time analysis method, (3) work sampling method, (4) time study, and (5) motion study. A complete description of these and other methods is beyond the scope of this book. Application of these techniques usually requires the skills of the industrial engineer. Health services organizations that are too small to employ such people can utilize the services of consultants in this area. Even so, in order that the manager in the health care setting has some understanding of these techniques and so that the manager can discuss them on an informed and intelligent basis with the industrial engineer, a brief discussion follows.

ANALYSIS OF PAST PRODUCTION RECORDS.   Perhaps this is the simplest method of measuring work and setting standards. Production records on the activities of the department can be maintained and analyzed. The manager can select the best past performance and use it as a standard on the assumption that if it was done before, the workers should be able to do it again. The advantages of this method are that it is easily used and at a relatively low cost with no need for highly trained personnel to administer it. The disadvantage is, of course, that existing inefficiencies are not corrected; they are merely recorded and analyzed.

THE TIME ANALYSIS METHOD.   This is a fairly simple method of establishing work standards. Various work activities done by an individual during the day are identified and placed on a form, then *the worker* records the actual time spent and units produced. The determination of a standard time from such information involves a great deal of subjectivity at best.

THE WORK SAMPLING METHOD.   This method is an improvement over the time analysis method in that a trained analyst makes random observations (based on statistical methods) of the various work activities done by individuals. The data thus obtained are more reliable than those from the time analysis method. However, they do require the services of a trained analyst.

TIME STUDY.   This method measures job performance to establish the time required for performing each operation at an average pace. The purpose is to measure the output of a worker of average skill who is performing his work with average effort under standardized conditions so that standard times can be determined. A job is divided into work elements or groupings of basic movements. Element times are taken directly at the work place by clock readings or remotely by motion picture analysis.

MOTION STUDY.   Its purpose is to make work performance easier and more productive by improving manual motions. The detailed motion study was originated by Frank B. Gilbreth at the end of the nineteenth century. He considered it a scientific method of eliminating wasted effort in work. He suggested that motion study consists of dividing work into the most fundamental elements possible, studying these elements separately and in relation to one another, and from these studies building methods of least waste.

It has been argued that in situations where the quality of patient care is involved these industrial engineering concepts should not be applied. It is much easier to accept them as part of the assembly line approach we have taken in manufacturing automobiles and washing machines. Clearly, the development and adherence to standards are *more* applicable in the manufacturing environment. Yet we should not discount them entirely as valuable tools in the health care organization. There are many situations where they are applicable. Broad-minded managers should be willing to try whatever tools and techniques they can to provide high quality care at the most reasonable cost.

A second important caution about setting standards involves the question of worker cooperation. The main purpose for setting any performance standard is to create effective goals for employees to work toward. This means that the standards are such that they can be achieved, and they should be considered fair by both the manager and his subordinates. Standards are more likely to be effective if they are set with the active participation of both manager and subordinates. Workers are more likely to accept them as reasonable and fair if they have had a part in their formulation.

Measuring Performance and Comparing to Standards

Once suitable standards have been set, the next steps in the control process can be taken. These consist of measuring actual performance and comparing it to standards that have been established. The manager does this by personally observing work and checking on his employees, and by analyzing summaries of data and reports submitted to him. Comparing information obtained in these ways with existing standards is a continuous daily function of the manager as he controls his area of responsibility.

There is no substitute for direct observation and personal contact by a manager in checking on employee performance. It is time consuming, but in addition to providing information for control purposes, it also permits the manager to make a continuous effort to improve the training and development of his employees. There is no better time to learn to do something correctly than just after it has been done incorrectly.

Whenever the manager observes his employees at work, he should assume a questioning attitude, but not necessarily a fault-finding one. He should not ignore mistakes, but the manner in which he questions is significant. He should ask whether or not there is any way in which he can help his employees do their jobs more easily, safely, or efficiently. Many standards are stated in general terms, but observations for control should look for specific instances such as inadequate output, sloppy work, or improperly performed jobs. At times it may be difficult to convince an employee that his work is generally unsatisfactory. But if reference can be made to specific cases, it is easier for the employee to recognize the deficiencies that may exist.

Another method available to the manager for checking on performance is the written report, which is especially important if the department is large or if it operates in several different locations. Reports should be clear, complete, concise, and correct. If a department or unit operates around the clock, as they so often do in health services organizations, the manager will have to depend, to a large extent, on written reports to appraise the performance of those shifts during which he is not usually present.

As the manager checks reports, he will find that many activities have been performed according to standard and can pass over these sections. He must concentrate on the exceptions—those activities where performance deviates from established standards. In many cases, the manager can practice what has been called the "exception principle." This means that he will request employees *not* to prepare reports on those activities which have attained preestablished standards, but merely to report on those items that are not up to the standard. After reviewing the reports, the manager can then take immediate action wherever it is needed. This approach works very well where employees are highly trained and professionalized.

Taking Corrective Action

The final step in the controlling function is taking corrective action. If there are no deviations from standard in the performance that has been taking place, then the controlling function is fulfilled by the first three steps. If, on the other hand, there are deviations, then the controlling function is not fulfilled until the final step of corrective action is accomplished. This means curbing undesirable results and bringing performance back into line. As we stated earlier, correction of deviations in performance is the point at which control coalesces with the other managerial functions of planning, organizing, directing, and coordinating.

Where deviations have occurred, the manager should first carefully check and analyze the facts in order to determine causes and reasons. Here he should bear in mind that standards were based on certain prerequisites, forecasts, and assumptions, which may not have materialized. A check may determine that the deviation was not caused by the employee in whose work it showed up. The corrective action must be directed toward the real source of the discrepancy. Other reasons for a deviation may be that the employee was not qualified. Additional training and supervision might help. There might be a situation where directions have not been given properly, and the employee was not well enough informed to do what was expected of him. Here the manager should again explain the standards which the employee is expected to maintain. These are only some of the reasons which may account for deviations from standards.

Only after a thorough analysis of the reasons for a deviation will the manager be in a position to take corrective action. He must decide what remedial action is necessary and what modifications will secure improved results in the future. Corrective action may consist of a revision of standards, a simple discussion, a verbal reprimand, or numerous other means of rectifying the situation. It may even consist of replacing certain employees. At times, serious forms of disciplinary action may have to be taken, particularly if major infractions of rules or policies are involved.

The manager, of course, must follow up and study the effect that each corrective action has on performance in the future. With further study and analysis, he may find that additional or different actions may be required to produce the desired results.

HUMAN REACTIONS TO CONTROLS

Ultimately, the success of a manager's attempt to control is determined by his effectiveness in getting people to make necessary modifications in their own performance. Although many managers assume that people will automatically act to correct their own behavior when directed to do so, this does not necessarily happen. Individuals may resist attempts to control them for a variety of reasons. Among them are the following:

1. It tends to disrupt a person's self-image.
2. The person fails to accept the organization's objectives.
3. An employee believes that the expected standard of perform-ance is too high.
4. He believes that standards are irrelevant to or, at least, an incomplete measurement of the organization's objectives.
5. A person may not object to the controls themselves, but to the assignment of control authority to particular people in the health services organization.
6. When informal group norms are consistent with control objec-tives, there will be a higher degree of acceptance of the control devices than when group norms are not consistent with control objectives.

Each of the reasons for resisting controls has its counterpart in a line of action that a manager might take to reduce the source of resistance. In addition to this, however, there is a general point of view which, when applied, enhances the likelihood that people will work toward the objectives of the control effort. It is this: in terms of personal acceptance of control procedures, it is generally the case that the more intimately a person is involved in the establishment of control standards, the more likely it is that he will accept them and try to measure up to them.

THE BUDGET AS A CONTROL DEVICE

The budget is a plan in that it expresses the projected activities of the health services organization or a unit of it in numerical terms covering a specified period of time. The use of the budget is a controlling function. Perhaps no better example than budgets could be found to illustrate the interrelatedness of planning and controlling as management functions. For this reason, we should devote some attention to them as control devices for the manager in the health care setting.

Budgets are the most general control devices the manager has to work with. Therefore, it is essential for a manager to be familiar with the general aspects of budget making and budget control. Budgets can be defined as preestablished standards to which operations are compared and adjusted through the exercise of control. A budget is a means of control insofar as it reflects the plan against which actual performance is measured. It provides information which enables the manager to take action, if necessary, to bring results into conformity with the plan.

The term *budgeting* usually refers to making a plan to cover operations for a definite period in the future. A budget states anticipated results in specific numerical terms. Although the terms usually are of a monetary nature, not all budgets are expressed in dollars and cents. There are also personnel budgets, which indicate the number of workers needed for each skill level and the number of man-hours allocated for certain activities.[2]

The making of a budget, whether it is financial or otherwise, contributes to improved planning, since budget plans must be quantified and stated specifically. Considerable effort is involved in budgeting, since it means that a manager must quantify his estimates about the future by attaching numerical values to specific plans. Figures placed in the final budget become the desired standard for achievement, thus becoming of vital concern and interest to the manager.

It is natural that people resent arbitrary standards; therefore, budgets should be established with the cooperation of those who are responsible for adhering to them. The manager should have an opportunity to participate in making the budget under which he is to work for the coming period. At the departmental level, the budget usually is established for one year, although it may be for a shorter period of time. Higher management may have other budgets that extend for some years in advance.

The most effective approach to budgeting in health services organizations is "bottom-up." Budgets should be initially prepared by those people who will implement them. The budgets are then sent up to higher level managers for approval (sometimes with adjustments). This approach has five distinct advantages:

1. Supervisors and department heads at the lower levels of responsibility have a more intimate view of their needs than those at the top.
2. Lower-level managers can provide more realistic breakdowns to support their proposals.
3. Managers are less likely to overlook some vital ingredient or hidden flaw that might subsequently impede implementation efforts if they develop the budgets for their own units.
4. Managers will be more strongly motivated to accept and meet budgets that they have had a hand in shaping.

---

[2]An excellent treatment of this subject can be found in Stephen H. Lipson and Mary D. Hensel, *Hospital Manpower Budget Preparation Manual* (Ann Arbor, MI: Health Administration Press, 1979).

5. Morale and satisfaction are usually higher when individuals par-
    ticipate actively in making decisions that affect them.[3]

Budgets are merely guides for management and not substitutes for good judgment. They should not be so detailed that
they become cumbersome. Further, budgets should allow the
manager some freedom to accomplish the objectives of his department with a reasonable degree of latitude and flexibility. To avoid
having it become a straitjacket, enlightened management will
assure flexibility of the budget by means of regular reviews so that
actual performance can be checked and compared against it. If
operating conditions have appreciably changed, and if there are
valid indications that the budget cannot be followed in the future, a
revision of the budget is in order.

Budgets do represent restrictions, and for this reason, some
managers do not like them. They may have a defensive approach to
budgets, an approach which has been acquired through painful
experience. Budgets represent a barrier to spending; they may
prohibit a raise in salary. Thus, in the minds of some managers and
employees, a budget becomes associated with "top management's
miserly behavior," rather than with planning and controlling vital
activities. The manager should try to understand that budgeting is
an orderly and disciplined approach to problems and that there is
enough flexibility built into a budget system to permit common
sense departures in order to serve the best interests of the health
services organization. Whatever can be done without a budget can
usually be done better with one.

The budgeting process if fairly complex, and its details are
beyond the scope of this book. However, the reader will find
Budgeting Procedures for Hospitals, a publication of the American
Hospital Association, an easy-to-read and valuable resource on the
budgeting process in health services organizations.[4]

PERFORMANCE APPRAISAL AS A CONTROL DEVICE

As we noted earlier in this chapter, control is effective only when it
guides someone's behavior. A very direct method of control over

---

[3]James A. F. Stoner, *Management* (Englewood Cliffs, NJ: Prentice-Hall, Inc., 1978),
p. 597. Reprinted by permission of Prentice-Hall, Inc., Englewood Cliffs, New
Jersey.

[4]An excellent treatment of budgeting can be found in Howard J. Berman and Lewis
E. Weeks, *The Financial Management of Hospitals,* 5th Edition (Ann Arbor, MI:
Health Administration Press, 1981).

individual employee's behavior, and one of the most important control mechanisms available to the manager, is the formal *performance appraisal* procedure. Performance appraisal is simply the feeding back to employees of information about how well they are performing their work for the health services organizations. While a great deal of this feedback occurs in the day-to-day interactions between managers and subordinates, we shall concentrate on the more formal annual or semi-annual appraisals.

In many health services organizations, these formal performance appraisals are based on personal characteristics (such as intelligence, creativity, punctuality, or ability to get along with peers) of the person being appraised. The actual appraisals usually consist of superiors rating their subordinates or sometimes a group of superiors (a committee) rating subordinates or even, on occasion, a group of peers rating a colleague. The common denominator in these traditional approaches is that the basis of the rating is the personal characteristics or traits of the person being appraised.

This traditional approach to performance appraisal often fails to improve the performance of employees. There is a growing concensus that a better method of appraisal can grow out of the MBO approach we discussed in Chapter 3. Recall that a central feature of MBO is periodic agreement between superior-subordinate pairs throughout the organization on the subordinate's objectives for a particular period. As was stated earlier in this chapter, the control function is intended to make certain that objectives are accomplished. This is true for the objectives at the level of the entire organization and for the departments and units that comprise it; but it is also true for each individual who works in the organization. Thus, a performance appraisal that uses the accomplishment of objectives by each individual as the criterion of performance can be very useful to the manager as a control device. In essence, the MBO approach is a *performance* based performance appraisal instead of a personal characteristic or trait based method. While the MBO approach to performance appraisal has not yet achieved widespread acceptance, it is increasingly being seen as a more useful approach to the appraisal of individual workers and as an effective device for controlling their contribution to the organizations in which they work. There is a growing literature base that supports this view.[5]

---

[5]See for example: Dale D. McConkey, *MBO for Nonprofit Organizations* (New York: AMACOM, 1975); Arthur X. Deegan, II, *Management by Objectives for Hospitals* (Germantown, MD: Aspen Systems Corporation, 1977).

However, there are difficulties with the MBO approach. For example, Kaluzny, et al. have noted that the approach requires:

a great deal of meeting time between superiors and subordinates, who already have extensive demands for actual service delivery activities. Usually, the process of defining goals and action plans is viewed as an appendage to existing work loads as opposed to an integrated part of activities. An exacerbating factor is that many of the objectives and activities associated with health service organizations are difficult to define, thus compounding the problems of establishing goals and specific activities.[6]

The budget and performance appraisal program are not the only control mechanisms available to the manager, but they are two of the most important ones. With this background on the control function of management, we can now turn our attention to *what* has to be controlled in health services organizations. As we noted earlier, everything that falls under the manager's responsibility is subject to control. However, we will limit our discussion to the two most pervasive and important areas of control: cost and quality of health services.

CONTROLLING COSTS

As we said at the outset of this chapter, in view of the limited resources our society allocates for the purpose of providing health services, those responsible for such services must make the most efficient use of resources. This translates itself directly into a concern for the cost of providing health services. Thus, controlling costs is one of the important aspects of the manager's role.

At the departmental or unit level costs can be broken down as follows: (1) payroll costs for departmental personnel, (2) the cost of supplies and services that must be purchased in order for the department to do its work, (3) capital investment in equipment, machines, and furniture, and (4) the more or less fixed costs of rent, utilities, taxes, insurance, and similar items where they apply. The first two elements of departmental costs suggested above are amenable to some managerial control. The last two lie largely outside of the departmental or unit manager's direct influence, although certain steps can be taken to control capital investment costs to a limited extent. Thus, the departmental manager who is

---

[6]Arnold D. Kaluzny, et al., *Management of Health Services* (Englewood Cliffs, NJ: Prentice-Hall, Inc., 1983), p. 251.

interested in controlling costs in his department must realize that he can have an effective impact on only *some* of the things that influence cost in his department.

We have stated that the control function consists of four steps: (1) establishing standards, (2) measuring performance, (3) comparing actual results with standards, and (4) correcting deviations from standards. In order to control personnel costs, standards must be set in the areas of number of personnel in the department, number of hours of overtime permitted, and amount of work to be done by each employee. As the work of the department progresses, actual performance can be checked against these standards. If deviations occur, then corrective action must be taken. In the area of personnel costs, deviations will either be in the number of personnel required or the amount of wok done by employees. Controlling the numbers of personnel or of overtime worked is relatively easy compared to controlling the amount of work. Nevertheless, if the manager finds that employees are not producing at the level established as a standard then something must be done. The first thing is, of course, to reevaluate the standard. It may very well be too high. If it is not, then the corrective action involves changing the manner in which employees perform their work. This is accomplished in a number of ways: (1) improving the manner in which the work is done through job analysis and work simplification, (2) training employees in the best way to perform the work, and (3) motivating employees to perform at maximum levels. These three things are synergistic in that their sum is greater than the sum of the parts—they reinforce each other. When applied together, they offer the manager a method of influencing departmental costs. Unfortunately, many times emphasis is placed on only one element (usually the manager's strong point) to the detriment of the others.

The costs of supplies and services must be controlled in much the same manner, i.e., establish standards, review actual results, compare to standards and, if necessary, take corrective action. The use of a supply budget can greatly facilitate this function. In fact, development and use of a tight but realistic departmental supply budget is the single most important thing the manager can do to control supply costs. Other useful steps include:

1. Centralize the issuance of supplies.
2. Develop a procedure for requisitioning supplies that will promote their appropriate use.
3. Issue supplies in sensible quantities.

As we suggested, the control of capital investment in equipment is not as amenable to control as personnel and supplies. However, the same control procedures are used. There are several suggestions that might be useful in controlling the equipment costs in a health services organization.

1. Purchase or lease only the equipment needed. A two-hundred-dollar adding machine may be quite adequate for certain uses, although it is not as appealing as the fancy microcomputer system.

2. Use and maintain the equipment properly. Be certain that all employees are trained in the proper use of machines. Make comparative studies of possible use of in-house service units for repair and maintenance of machines instead of outside, contracted service agreements.

3. Standardize the equipment because this will simplify training and maintenance and may result in quantity discounts in the original lease or purchase.

4. Replace machines whenever this will result in a real cost saving through increased productivity.

THE MANAGEMENT AUDIT AS A MEANS OF CONTROLLING

The manager in a health services organization very often experiences a problem common to managers in all organizations. This is the problem of being so involved in the day-to-day operation that he cannot see the opportunities for improvement all around him. The manager who has a heavy workload finds it difficult, especially where there are no obvious problems, to make changes in the present operations and procedures. However, the effective manager should have a personal objective of constantly seeking to improve utilization of those resources entrusted to him. This attitude spurs him to continuously seek better and more efficient ways of getting things done.

A tool that can be of great value to the manager in the health services organization who is trying to control costs (as well as make general improvements in his department's operation) is the management audit. This is nothing more than a *systematic analysis* of activities in the manager's department or unit. Such an audit can yield results that lead to cost control as well as general improvement in departmental operations. The objectives of a management audit are to bring into sharp focus the activities and operations of the department and to force a careful appraisal of the effectiveness and efficiency of work performance. A management audit permits the manager to review the organizational pattern, sharpen objectives, reemphasize policies, review standards, and scrutinize procedures. It is hardly possible that such a close analysis of any department or unit in a health services organization would not uncover areas where improvements can be made.

The manager will probably conduct the audit, although, if possible, an outside consultant can be of great value. After all, the performance of the manager is one of the key areas of interest in the audit. Whoever does conduct it must remember that its purpose is to gather facts, develop recommendations, and work toward implementing them. These ends should be accomplished accurately, effectively, and expeditiously. The key to an effective management audit is the thought that goes into it before it is conducted. The management audit can be very extensive or relatively simple, depending on the manager's time and the objectives he sets.

In essence, the management audit is conducted by analyzing in a systematic and planned way the work done in a particular department. Such a searching approach to the effectiveness and efficiency of operations will take time and effort. The results, however, make it worthwhile. Three general benefits are obtained from the management audit.

1. *Evaluation of operations.* This is an obvious benefit in that a systematic examination of all phases of operation within the department or unit is made.

2. *A means of effective control.* When the audit is made, the manager has at his disposal a significant tool for control. Remember that control implies establishing standards, measuring actual results, and then correcting deviations. The information obtained in the management audit goes far beyond the few pieces of quantifiable information usually used for control purposes in most health organization departments. It provides comprehensive information on what actual performance is like in the department or unit.

3. *Improvement of relationships between the manager and his subordinates.* As employees in the department learn how an audit works and how everyone benefits, a better feeling develops. Management sees its plans and directives carried out. A greater understanding arises, for each employee sees his particular job in its relationship to the jobs of others,

discovers how each job fits into the total pattern, and learns the contributions of each job and worker to the whole departmental operation.

These benefits can only be realized if the management audit is properly conceived and carried out and if the findings are communicated to all workers in the department. Of course, the burden of responsibility falls on the manager to use the information gathered to make improvements that can lead to effective cost control and a general improvement in operations within the department.

Some authorities suggest periodic audits, usually annually. However, the scope of the management audit suggested above dictates that a more realistic approach is for the manager in the health services organization to be involved in one aspect or another of the audit on a continuing basis. What this means is that the manager will always be involved in a systematic and careful examination of what is going on around him. The management audit gives him a framework within which the analysis is conducted. The end result is a constant searching for areas where improvements can be made, and for more effective control of the resources over which he has been given responsibility.

CONTROLLING THE QUALITY OF CARE

Few subjects in the health services field have received as much attention as the quality of care provided. This interest stems basically from the professional concern of those who deliver care to do so in the best possible manner. In recent years, more formalized interest in quality of care has come from major third party payers (primarily the federal government) and consumer groups who have begun to realize that the care they receive is subject to variations in quality. The tremendous increase in malpractice suits has served to emphasize the interest in and concern about the quality of care provided in health services organizations.

There are many aspects involved in measuring quality of medical care.[7] For example, one can measure and evaluate the *structure* of the setting in which care is given by looking at the characteristics of the setting that are thought to be related to

---

[7]For an excellent treatment of this subject see: Avedis Donabedian, "Evaluating the Quality of Medical Care," *Milbank Memorial Fund Quarterly*, XLIV, July 1966.

quality. These might include the scope of services offered, the education of those providing the services, or any of a number of other structural characteristics thought to be related to quality. The actual *process* of providing care can be examined by looking at the interactions between patients and those providing care. This is accomplished by such means as direct observation of medical practice, medical record review, and a determination of the appropriateness of treatment. A final aspect of quality that can be measured is the *outcome* of care. That is, the status of the patient after care has been provided, or the end result, can be evaluated. For the health services organization as a whole, such things as adjusted death rate, infection rate, and disability rate can serve as a means of measuring outcome.

While there is neither universal agreement on how to control quality in health services organizations, nor how to measure quality, there is widespread acceptance that it should receive considerable attention. In the case of hospitals, the Joint Commission on Accreditation of Hospitals (JCAH) has established as one of its standards that "the hospital shall demonstrate that the quality of care provided to all patients is consistently optimal by continuously evaluating it through reliable and valid measures."[8] An excellent description of the JCAH's "Performance Evaluation Procedure for Auditing and Improving Patient Care" has been developed by Jacobs, Christoffel, and Dixon.[9]

The American Hospital Association has developed a guide for use by hospitals in developing their quality assurance efforts.[10] The basic framework of this guide is very much like the four-step control model we developed earlier in this chapter. The steps in the quality assurance program outlined by the American Hospital Association are as follows:[11]

Step A - Criteria development
Step B - Description of the actual practice
Step C - Judgment or evaluation (does B = A?)
Step D - Corrective action (necessary if B ≠ A)
Step E - Reassessment (after D, now does B = A?)

---

[8]Joint Commission on Accreditation of Hospitals periodically revises its standards, the latest being in 1980.

[9]Charles M. Jacobs, Tom H. Christoffel, and Nancy Dixon, *Measuring the Quality of Patient Care: The Rationale for Outcome Audit* (Cambridge, MA: Ballinger Publishing Company, 1976).

[10]American Hospital Association, *Quality Assurance Program for Medical Care in Hospitals* (Chicago: American Hospital Association, 1972).

[11]*Ibid.*, Section 3, p. 1.

In applying the general outline of the controlling function (setting standards, measuring actual results, comparing to standards, taking corrective action), one must first develop standards of quality. These will be characteristics of excellence against which the actual care being provided will be measured. The difficulties in setting appropriate standards makes this one of the most complex issues facing health services managers.

If the professionals in the health services organization can agree on standards, measure the actual results of the provision of care, compare them to the standards, and take corrective actions when necessary, then they will be controlling the quality of care. Health services organizations are doing this to some extent. For example, hospitals typically have a utilization review program and a medical audit program in which peers evaluate the care that is given in the hospital. The fact that these procedures are peer reviews is important because peers can best determine the standards that are appropriate. Also, peer judgment is necessary in evaluation of the actual care provided, and peers can best determine the appropriate corrective action that needs to be taken.

It is fair to say that, at this point in time, controlling the quality of care provided in health services organizations is receiving a great deal of attention and effort. The complexities involved in determining appropriate standards are the major drawback. Until such time as widely accepted standards are developed and disseminated, the control of quality of care in health services organizations will not be as complete as health professionals want it to be.

CONTROLLING IS DIFFICULT

The reader can see from the examples of controlling costs and quality of care in health services organizations that this is one of the most difficult functions of the manager. The following suggestions reflect some of the most important requirements of effective controls:

1. *Controls must reflect the nature and needs of the activity.* All control systems should reflect the job they are to perform. This is merely a requirement of reflection of plans: the more that controls are designed to deal with and reflect the specific nature and structure of plans, the more effectively they will serve the interests of the health services organization.

2. *Controls should report deviations promptly.* The ideal control system detects deviations soon after they actually occur. Only

if information reaches the manager in a timely manner can he or she take effective action.

3. *Controls should be forward looking.* Although ideal control is instantaneous, as in certain electronic controls, the facts of managerial life include a time lag between the deviation and corrected action. Perhaps the key point of control in ensuring achievement of objectives is that of detecting potential or actual deviation from plans early enough to permit effective corrective action. Therefore, the manager, in striving to apply this principle, would surely prefer a forecast of what will probably happen next week or next month—even though this contains a margin of error—to a report, accurate to several decimal points, of the past about which he can do nothing.

4. *Controls should be objective.* Management necessarily has many subjective elements in it, but whether a subordinate is doing a good job should ideally not be a matter for subjective determination. Where controls are subjective, a manager's or a subordinate's personality may influence judgments of performance inaccurately. However, people have difficulty explaining away objective control of their performance, particularly if the standards and measurements are kept up to date through periodic review. Effective control requires objective, accurate, and suitable standards.

5. *Controls should be flexible.* Controls must remain workable in the face of changed plans, unforeseen circumstances, or outright failures. If they are to remain effective, despite failure or changes in plans, flexibility is required in their selection.

6. *Controls should point up exceptions at critical points.* Effective control requires attention to those factors critical to performance. Generally, the more a manager concentrates his control efforts on exceptions, the more efficient will be the results of his control.

7. *Controls should be economical.* Controls must be worth their cost. Although this requirement is simple, its practice is often complex, for a manager may find it difficult to know what a particular control system is worth, or to know what it costs. Economy is relative, since the benefits vary with the importance of the activity, the size of the operation, the expense that might be incurred in the absence of control, and the contribution the system can make.

8. *Controls should be understandable.* Some control systems, especially those based upon mathematical formulas, complex break-even charts, detailed analyses, and computer simulations are not always understandable to the managers who

must use them. Sometimes the manager could understand them if he would take the time to learn to do so; but whether his lack of understanding results from complex techniques or impatience in learning them, the effect is the same: the control system will not function.

9. *Controls should lead to corrective action.* A control system that detects deviations from plans will be little more than an interesting exercise if it does not show the way to corrective action. An adequate system will disclose where failures are occurring and who is responsible for them, so that corrective action can be taken.

10. *Controls should reflect the organization pattern.* Organization structure, being the principal vehicle for coordinating the work of people, is also a major means for maintaining control. It is the manager who is the focal point of control, just as he is the focal point for the assignment of tasks and the delegation of authority and responsibility.

Among the most innovative ideas which, if properly used, can assist managers in controlling both costs and quality in their areas of responsibility is the idea of Quality Circles. These are small-group, problem-oriented meetings in which *employees* focus on work-related problems. "Quality Cicles have been found to enhance the quality of patient care and services, reduce errors, build an attitude of problem prevention, improve communications, and inspire more effective teamwork in the hospital."[12] The key to effective Quality Circles is management commitment. Employees often have deeper knowledge of their specific jobs than their managers; when managers create an atmosphere in which employees are rewarded for their ideas (through recognition, promotion, pay increases) they often find them contributing valuable solutions to ongoing problems.

SUMMARY

Controlling is the regulation of activities in accordance with the requirements of plans. Controlling consists of four steps: (1) establishing standards, (2) measuring performance, (3) comparing actual results with standards, and (4) correcting deviations from standards.

---

[12]American Hospital Association, *Hospitals*, October 1, 1982, p. 72.

There are different types of standards and there are a number of techniques that can be useful in setting them. The manager's personal observation is the best way of measuring performance. If the manager finds that corrective action is necessary, he should view it as a means of improving the performance of his subordinates. He should keep in mind that, generally, the more intimately a person is involved in the control decisions that are made, the more likely it is that he will accept them and support them.

Controlling costs is a process that the manager can undertake to improve the effectiveness with which his or her department utilizes its resources. The more complex issue of controlling the quality of care provided in the health services organization has become increasingly important in recent years.

Managing Change: The Management Imperative

TEN

The Hospital Administrator looked slowly around the lecture hall at the students. He was very pleased to have been invited to be a guest lecturer for the nursing students on the topic of "Management in the Hospital." He cleared his throat and began.

"My subject this afternoon is management. Some of you may not find it as interesting as the professional practice of nursing, but it is just as important to the well-being of the patient as any of the other skills that go into modern medical care ..."

The Administrator continued lecturing for almost an hour and a half before saying, "In conclusion, the single greatest challenge facing the manager is to look at the organization, or that part of it he or she manages, and think about what is—compared to what should be—and then find ways to change it."

As he watched the students file out of the lecture hall, he collected his notes and thought to himself, "Bringing about change really is the key to management—but it's so much easier to talk about than to do. That situation with Luther Fillerey pointed up half a dozen things that needed to be changed. Oh well, I'll get to them soon."

It was 3:30 p.m. as the Administrator headed back to his office and the pile of work waiting for him.

INTRODUCTION

Change is not easy, nor has it ever been. Machiavelli wrote in *The Prince* several hundred years ago that "it must be said that there is nothing more difficult to carry out, nor more doubtful in success, than to initiate a new thing." Those of us involved in trying to improve the delivery of health services know the truth of Machiavelli's words. Yet if the objective of making health care available and affordable to all is to be realized, changes must occur. Bringing about change is the basic imperative faced by all managers in health services organizations.

Health services organizations are under unprecedented pressure to change—in some cases to change their methods of operation, in some csaes to change their objectives, and in some cases to change both. These pressures stem from consumers and their advocates, government, leaders in the medical establishment, and a growing awareness on the part of many people (inside and outside health services organizations) that they, as institutions, are not as effective as they need to be. The force of these pressures is exacerbated by continuing progress in medical science and technology, which outstrips the system for delivering health services. It is clear to the knowledgeable observer that the delivery system is being restructured and the roles of health professionals are being redefined in modern society. However, as Burns has pointed out, organizations usually exist in a state of equilibrium. Organizations generate numerous forces and balances to perpetuate themselves and to reject changes that disturb the equilibrium.[1]

There are many types of changes that take place within health services organizations. A very important dichotomy of these changes is whether they are imposed on the organization (by a government regulation for example) or made without direct coercive, external pressure. Both situations are organizational changes,

---

[1]J. M. Burns, *Leadership* (New York: Harper and Row, 1978), p. 416.

but the latter is an *innovative* organizational change. We are more concerned here with the innovative than with the imposed change. Health services organizations do not exist in a vacuum. They interact with, react to, and influence their environments. The health services organization which only reacts to its environment (where changes are literally forced by external pressures) cannot be thought of as an innovative organization. We shall restrict our definition to innovative organizational change. We should point out at the outset that there is not yet a universally accepted definition of innovative organizational change.

Thompson defines innovation as "the generation, acceptance, and implementation of new ideas, processes, products, and services."[2] Becker and Whisler separate the creation of an idea from its use. They define innovation as "the first or early use of an idea by one of a set of organizations with similar goals."[3] The first or early user is thus the innovator, regardless of the source of the idea. Mohr separates invention from use, but does not include first or early use in his definition. He defines innovation as "the successful introduction into an applied situation of means or ends that are new to that situation."[4] The reader can see that these three representative definitions of innovation are quite different.

One of the best definitions is suggested by Rowe and Boise. They state: "Organizational innovation refers to the successful utilization of processes, programs, or products which are new to an organization and which are introduced as a result of decisions made within that organization."[5] Using this definition, it is possible to distinguish between organization change and innovative organizational change. When change is forced from external pressures, it can be defined as the successful utilization of processes, programs, or products which are new to an organization. If, on the other hand, the change comes about because of decisions made within the organization then it is *innovative* organization change and not merely change. Innovation and change are both important concepts for the health professional manager because they are both taking place and will continue to take place in the health services organization.

---

[2]Victor A. Thompson, "Bureaucracy and Innovation," *Administrative Science Quarterly,* June 1966, p. 2.

[3]Selwyn W. Becker and Thomas L. Whisler, "The Innovative Organization: A Selective View of Current Theory and Research," *The Journal of Business,* October 1967, p. 462.

[4]Lawrence B. Mohr, "Determinants of Innovation in Organizations," *The American Political Science Review,* March 1967, p. 112.

[5]Lloyd A. Rowe and William B. Boise, *Organizational and Managerial Innovation: A Reader* (Pacific Palisades, CA: The Goodyear Publishing Company, 1973), p. 6.

If one observes a number of organizational changes in health care settings, a variety of objectives would seem to be present. These objectives might be such things as better performance, greater motivation, reduced turnover, or any one of an almost limitless number of things. However, in health care settings organizational changes usually fit into one of two broader categories: (1) changes in the organization's level of adaptation to its environment and (2) changes in the internal behavior patterns of participants. Health services organizations are in a constant struggle to adapt themselves to their external environment. They cannot control (except to a very limited extent) the external environment; therefore, organizational changes are required to allow the organization to deal with challenges imposed from outside the organization by such things as consumer demands, government regulation, medical and scientific advances, planning agencies, third party payors, and so forth. For the most part, health services organizations make organizational changes in reaction to these environmental pressures. In some cases, however, changes are made without outside pressure or in anticipation of future pressures. This innovative behavior characterizes organizations that lead instead of follow their industry. Such health services organizations can be seen as attempting to change their environments as well as themselves.

Obviously, if an organization's level of adaptation is to be improved, the behavior patterns of a number of employees must be modified both in terms of their relationships to each other and to their jobs. Thus the second basic category of organizational change is that which alters the behavior patterns of organization participants.

BRINGING ABOUT ORGANIZATIONAL CHANGE

Organizational change, whether it represents an innovation or is imposed by pressures external to the organization, can be introduced by a number of approaches. A useful dichotomy of the various approaches is to look at those that emphasize *what* is to be changed and those that emphasize the process of *how* change is introduced.

One of the most widely used delineations of the *what* approaches is that made by Leavitt.[6] He describes three approaches

[6]Harold J. Leavitt, "Applied Organization Change in Industry: Structural, Technological, and Human Approaches," in *New Perspectives in Organization Research* (New York: John Wiley and Sons, Inc., 1964).

to organizational change: structure, technology, and people. Structural approaches to the introduction of change are such things as the organization chart, budgeting methods, and rules and regulations. The technological approaches stress changes introduced by such means as the introduction of new services (open heart surgery, for example) or new technological equipment (CAT scanners, for example). The third classification, the people approaches, stresses alterations in attitudes, motivation, and behavioral skills. Changes of this type are made through such techniques as training programs, selection procedures, and performance appraisal programs.

A good illustration of *how* approaches is contained in Greiner's work identifying seven approaches to change most frequently used by managers.[7]

A. *Unilateral Power*:
1. *The Decree Approach*. A "one-way" announcement originating with a person with high formal authority and passed on to those in lower positions.
2. *The Replacement Approach*. Individuals in one or more key organizational positions are replaced by other individuals. The basic assumption is that organizational changes are a function of a key person's ability.
3. *The Structural Approach*. Instead of decreeing or injecting new blood into work relationships, management changes the required relationships of subordinates working in the situation. By changing the structure of organizational relationships, organizational behavior is also presumably affected.
B. *Shared Power*:
4. *The Group Decision Approach*. Here we have participation by group members in selecting from several alternative solutions specified in advance by superiors. This approach involves neither problem identification nor problem solving, but emphasizes the obtaining of group agreement to a particular course of action.
5. *The Group Problem Solving Approach*. Problem identification and problem solving through group discussion. Here the group has wide latitude, not only over choosing the problems to be discussed, but then in developing solutions to these problems.
C. *Delegated Power*:
6. *The Data Discussion Approach*. Presentation and feedback of relevant data to the client system either by a change catalyst or by change agents within the [health care organization]. Organizational members are encouraged to develop their own analyses of the data, presented in the form of case materials, survey findings, or data reports.

---

[7]Larry E. Greiner, "Patterns of Organization Change," *Harvard Business Review,* May-June, 1967. (Copyright 1967 by the President and Fellows of Harvard College; all rights reserved.)

7. *The Sensitivity Training Approach.* Managers are trained in small discussion groups to be more sensitive to the underlying processes of individual and group behavior. Changes in work patterns and relationships are assumed to follow from changes in interpersonal relationships. Sensitivity approaches focus upon interpersonal relationships first, then hope for, or work toward, improvements in work performance.

It should be noted that few changes can be successfully introduced using only one of these strategies. A balanced approach carefully combining several elements is needed. For example, a health professional manager may wish to encourage a more effective communication network among his subordinates. To accomplish this change he will need to take a "people" approach by providing the subordinates with a training program in communication skills. However, the full implementation of this change may also require "structural" changes that lead to more open communication among the subordinates.

In an analysis of eighteen studies of organizational change, it was discovered that successful changes utilized patterns involving sharing approaches; that is, superiors sought participation of subordinates in decision making. In the less successful attempts, the approaches were closer to either end of the continuum outlined above; five used unilateral approaches of decree, replacement, and structure, and two used sensitivity training or fact-finding and discussion.[8]

Organizational change is a very complex process. The manager concerned with introducing, managing, and responding to such change needs a conceptual framework of its process. Most research indicates that the central concept needed to see the process of change clearly and objectively is to think of organizational change as an evolving series of stages. It does not occur all at once. Rather, one phase sets necessary conditions for moving into subsequent stages. Lewin pioneered in identifying three phases of change: unfreezing, changing, and refreezing.[9] The unfreezing stage represents a necessary first step in stimulating people to recognize the need for change. The changing stage involves introduction and application of the change. Finally, the refreezing stage provides the necessary reinforcement to make certain that new behavior patterns are adopted on a permanent basis.

---

[8]*Ibid.*, p. 125.
[9]Kurt Lewin, "Group Decision and Social Change," T. Newcomb and E. Hartley (eds.) *Readings in Social Psychology* (New York: Holt, Rinehart, and Winston, Inc., 1947.)

No matter what change process is used, there are several prerequisites to organizational change:[10]

1. Something has to precipitate change—a happening, development, signal, or an individual has to place the organization in a mold for change.

2. The organization itself must be ready to change, or someone within the organization, the change agent, must convince others that old, comfortable ways should be replaced by new, untried ways.

3. The proposed new ways either must mesh with or not seriously disturb the existing value system.

4. The change agent must select the approach or combination of approaches necessary to convince others of the need for change (for example, by planting seeds for change through a board/management/medical staff educational process and/or by using task forces and other internal devices to develop ideas and build coalitions).

5. The change agent must create a shared body of values and attitudes—a new consensus where key individuals within an organization reinforce one another in selling the new way and in defending it against inertia, reluctance, or outright opposition.

THE HUMAN ELEMENT IN CHANGE

Some changes involve a new design for a form or a new machine; others involve basic behavior patterns in people. But *all* change affects people in the organization in some way. Regardless of who may institute the change, the person affected is compelled. The person's response is a function of both background, including needs and experiences, and the particular situation in which the change is introduced. One cannot predict from the technical content alone the person's response. A manager may view change "logically" and feel that any resistance is irrational. But he will never understand or be able to predict change responses unless something is known about the person affected by it and about that person's past experiences.

---

[10]Joseph P. Peters and Simone Tseng, "Managing Strategic Change," *Hospitals*, June 1, 1983, p. 65.

Each changed situation is interpreted by an individual according to his attitudes. The way that he feels about the change then determines how he will respond to it. Attitudes, in turn, are not the result of chance: they are caused. One cause is personal history, which refers to a person's biological processes, his background, and all his social experiences away from work. That is what he brings to the work place. A second cause is the work environment itself, reflecting the fact that he is a group member and is influenced by its codes, patterns, and attitudes.

The human element is, by its nature, complex. For the manager wishing to make a substantive change this complexity requires a comprehensive and systematic approach to change. A variety of tools and techniques must be used. The term for such an approach is *organization development* (OD). Huse defines OD as:

> . . . a process by which behavioral science principles and practices are used in an ongoing organization in a planned and systematic way to attain such goals as developing greater organizational competence, bringing about organization improvement, improving the quality of work life, and improving organizational effectiveness. . . . The focus includes the motivation, utilization, and integration of human resources within the organization.[11]

This systematic approach increases the likelihood that change can be successfully accomplished. Yet, even with such efforts, change is often difficult to achieve. As we see below, this is largely because of the human propensity to resist change.

The Human Response to Change— Resistance

One of the most persistent problems faced by a manager attempting to initiate a change is resistance. There are a number of possible sources for this often-encountered attitude. These sources include the following:[12]

1. Insecurity
2. Possible social loss
3. Possible economic loss

---

[11]Edgar F. Huse, *Organization Development and Changes, 2nd Edition* (New York: West, 1980), p. 3.

[12]Edwin B. Flippo and Gary M. Munsinger, *Management: A Behavioral Approach* (Boston: Allyn and Bacon, 1978), p. 527.

4. Stability of the situation

5. Impact upon other portions of the organization

6. Inconvenience

7. The labor union

Sources of Resistance

Perhaps a few words about each of these sources of resistance to change is in order.

INSECURITY.   Insecurity is usually suggested as the major source of general resistance. The present is known, understood, and has been absorbed. There is comfort in the *status quo;* people have worked out a relationship with it. Change introduces some degree of uncertainty. Organizations are often so complex that a seemingly simple change, such as moving the location of the water cooler, can have far-reaching repercussions. To some, such a move is a symbol of management's unconcern for inconvenienced employees. To others, it means more traffic and interference around their work place. And to still others, it is another bit of evidence of the autocracy of management. Change, then, could involve a reduction in a current level of satisfaction. The changee often does not really know what will happen, but his past experiences have taught him to look for the worst. Change also suggests that either he or his methods are unsatisfactory, and thus he is condemned.

SOCIAL LOSSES.   There are various kinds of social losses that can ensue from change. The mere fact that management wishes to impose a change is evidence of the employee's lack of independence. In addition, many of the modern technological changes tend to isolate the employee from co-workers even further.

Change will also involve altering informal relationships among personnel. A close friend may now work in another room, or work materials may now be received from a person of lower status. The complex of informal relationships must inevitably be affected by the introduction of any change involving people. Established status symbols may be destroyed, or a lower status individual may be given a high status symbol. Social acceptance will be in jeopardy if a particular employee is favorable toward a change inaugurated by management while the majority of the group is not. The individual may have to choose between cooperation with management and the friendship of co-workers. Thus what may seem desirable from a logical and technical view may meet with heavy resistance because the price in social relationships is too high.

ECONOMIC LOSSES.   There are many changes introduced by management that inflict economic loss upon employees. In many cases, through technological advances, more work can now be done by the same or fewer personnel. Resistance to this kind of change is entirely understandable and most difficult to overcome. Even without the loss of job, change raises the possibility of reduced earnings, or of the same earnings accompanied by an accelerated pace or increased contribution.

STABILITY.   If the organization's past history has been highly stable, it is doubly difficult to introduce a change. When personnel have not only adjusted to the *status quo,* but have begun to feel that it is a permanent situation, the inauguration of even the most minor change is considered to be revolutionary and highly disruptive. There are times, of course, when an organization that has pursued a policy of instituting changes fairly frequently has, in this manner, made change a part of the *status quo.*

IMPACT ON THE ORGANIZATION.   Few if any changes can be kept completely isolated; there are usually repercussions felt by other parts of the organization. These affected areas may bring about the downfall of the proposed improvement. For example, there is often a desire to change and improve supervisory practices; supervisors are therefore given a training course in human relations. Effecting changes in supervisory attitudes and methods is difficult enough; visualize, then, the difficulties the supervisors in turn experience upon returning from the training course. Their subordinates had previously worked out a relationship with these superiors; now they do not know what to expect. The most admirable and correct action by the newly trained supervisor is likely to be met with a great deal of suspicion, particularly if it is inconsistent with the pattern of the past. Many attempts to change supervisory behavior have met with failure because other parts of the organization have been neglected.

INCONVENIENCE.   There is in any change a certain amount of inconvenience and extra effort required to make the adjustment. Old habits must be unlearned and new practices assimilated. Thus inconvenience is a factor which will stimulate some resistance, but it is not the most fundamental source of opposition.

THE UNION.   If there is a labor union, its representatives are at times inclined to oppose on principle any change suggested by management regardless of the merits of the proposal. These representatives were not elected necessarily to cooperate with management and staff officials; their role is to protect the interests of the union member. The employee is usually more comfortable with a fighting union representative than with one inclined to cooperate with management on changes designed to promote the interests of the organization. Thus it is expected that the union will produce some resistance, even in cases where union leaders recognize that proposed changes are good both for union members and the health services organization.

Looking for the Causes of Resistance

As the foregoing indicates, the causes of resistance to change are many and complex. It is much easier to be aware of the symptoms than of the underlying causes. There may be increased griping by employees and suggestions that the change will not work. Even more dangerous symptoms may show up as poor work, slowdowns, or other factors. If the health professional manager views the symptoms as fundamental problems, he or she will be at a loss in attempting to resolve the situation. For example, the many reasons given as to why the change will never work can be discussed and most, if not all, of them diminished through rational analysis. Yet it soon becomes apparent that the real source of resistance has to do less with rational analysis than with intuitive feelings. If management never attempts to ascertain the source of these feelings, it will constantly be treating the symptom rather than the causes.

Figure 10-1 illustrates the manner in which individuals respond to change.

STEPS IN MAKING A CHANGE

Given the background on resistance to change described above, how can the manager implement changes? The following approach can be effective. It is a step-by-step method that includes the feature of encouraging the participation of employees who will be affected by the change.

Step 1. Recognition of the Need for Change

This step is crucial to the entire change process. It is at this point that managers decide to act. If, in the manager's judgment, the forces for change are significant, the process moves to the next step—diagnosis.

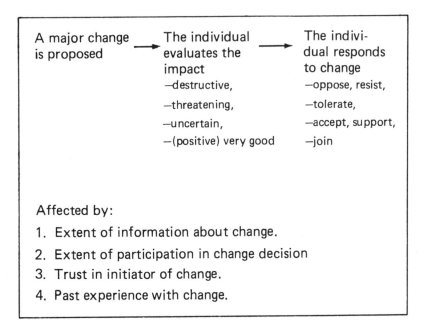

Figure 10–1. An individual's response to change.

SOURCE: Robert M. Fulmer, *The New Management* (Macmillan Publishing Co., Inc., 1974), p. 418.

Step 2. Diagnosis of the Problem

The key decision in this step is whether the stimulus for change should be acted upon. This decision can be approached by making three related decisions. (The reader may wish to review the material on decision making in Chapter 4 at this point.)

1. What is the problem as distinct from its symptoms?

2. What must be changed to resolve the problem?

3. What outcomes are expected and how will these outcomes be measured?

The managerial response to these questions should be stated in terms of criteria that reflect organizational effectiveness. Measurable outcomes such as production, efficiency, satisfaction, adaptiveness, and development must be linked to skill, attitudinal, behavioral, and structural changes necessitated by the problem identification. It is necessary to make changes in response to a real situation requiring a change and not on the whim of the manager or anyone else.

Step 3. Identification of Alternative Methods and Strategies

In this step, the health professional manager considers the possible approaches to change that are available to him. At this point he must take into account the needs of his employees as well as of the health services organization. The individual situation will dictate the possible approaches to take. Inherent in the situational approach is the understanding that each organization must adapt in unique ways to its particular situation. Accordingly, conditions are created that limit the range of possible methods and strategies available to the manager. The leadership style, the formal organization, and group norms all are constraints or limitations that must be considered.

Step 4. Selection of the Method and Strategy

The analysis of the problem, identification of alternatives, and recognition of constraints lead to the selection of the most promising method and strategy. At this point, the judgment of the health professional manager is the key factor. He must select an approach to change that he feels is most likely to yield the desired results. It is very important to let the people who will be affected by the change participate in the choice.

Step 5. Implementation of the Change

This is, of course, the critical step. It is also the most difficult because at this point one stops thinking about the change and actually makes it. The following are some suggestions that will prove helpful:

1. Make certain that employees understand the situation that makes a change necessary. If they can perceive its necessity, they are more likely to make an effort to adjust.

     It is often advisable for a change to be introduced on a trial basis in order to encourage acceptance. Familiarity, through experience, with the nature of the change, as well as the assurance that one is not stuck with it, may reduce some of the insecurity. The manager must also appreciate the importance of allowing enough time for the change to be digested.

2. Disturb as little as possible the existing customs and informal relationships. The culture developed by a group has real value from the viewpoint of organizational effectiveness, and management should work in consonance with these beliefs when possible.

3. Provide information about the change in advance. Such information can include the reasons necessitating the change, its nature, timing, and impact upon the organization and the people in it.

4. Encourage employee participation in the implementation (as well as the formation) of changes. A number of studies have suggested that participation in the determination and implementation of change will reduce resistance. There is a feeling of lessened pressure upon employees and greater understanding of the nature and probable impact of the change. There is also likely to be an increased sense of pride since the change was worked out through consultative practices. It is clear that people follow their own decisions best.

5. Provide for means of releasing tensions resulting from the introduction of change. In many cases, change results in the creation of tensions among those affected by it. Management should be aware of the necessity for the release of these emotional tensions. It should not attempt to meet hostility with hostility, nor emotions with logic. After the resentment has been aired, it is then possible that employees may finally accept the change.

Step 6. Evaluating the Change

Evaluation is necessitated by the health professional manager's responsibility to utilize optimally the resources entrusted to him or her and to account for their utilization. Additionally, evaluation provides feedback, which can lead to corrections where necessary or can strengthen the manager's conviction that the change was wise—or it can create the recognition that further change is necessary.

Change is not easy—certainly not as easy as outlining six steps might lead one to believe. But it is inevitable and it is necessary. It might very well be that the most important skill the manager in a health services organization can possess is the skill to implement changes. When one looks at our health services organizations and sees what is, compared to what should be, the importance of change comes into focus.

SUMMARY

This chapter looks at the management imperative of change—
innovative change, which is the successful utilization of processes,
programs, or products that are new to an organization and are
introduced as a result of decisions made within that organization.

Change is not easy. People resist it for many reasons: insecurity, the possibility of social and economic loss, and other reasons.
Changes can be wrought in many ways. Some are more successful
than others and these are pointed out in this chapter. The process
of change can be viewed as a step-by-step approach consisting of:

1. Recognition of the need for change.
2. Diagnosis of the problem.
3. Identification of alternative methods and strategies.
4. Selection of the method and strategy.
5. Implementation of the change.
6. Evaluation of the change.

Alfred North Whitehead has said, "The art of progress is to
preserve order amid change and to preserve change amid order."
Clearly, this is a skill that will well serve the health professional, who
is also a manager, in the years ahead.

Index